Asa Hull

Temperance Rallying Songs

consisting of a large variety of solos, quartettes, and choruses, suited to every

phase of the great temperance reformation

Asa Hull

Temperance Rallying Songs
consisting of a large variety of solos, quartettes, and choruses, suited to every phase of the great temperance reformation

ISBN/EAN: 9783337265717

Printed in Europe, USA, Canada, Australia, Japan

Cover: Foto ©Thomas Meinert / pixelio.de

More available books at **www.hansebooks.com**

TEMPERANCE
RALLYING SONGS

Consisting of a large variety of

SOLOS, QUARTETTES, AND CHORUSES, SUITED TO EVERY

PHASE OF THE

GREAT TEMPERANCE REFORMATION

BY

ASA HULL

Author of "Hull's Temperance Glee Book," "Hull's Chorus Book," "Gem of Gems," "Jewels of Praise," "Gospel Praise Book," etc.

NEW YORK

PUBLISHED BY ASA HULL, 150 NASSAU STREET

BOSTON	CHICAGO
OLIVER DITSON & CO.	LYON & HEALY
PHILADELPHIA	CINCINNATI
J. E. DITSON & CO.	THE JOHN CHURCH CO.

SAN FRANCISCO
REV. JOHN D. HAMMOND

PREFACE

TEMPERANCE RALLYING SONGS, is our contribution to help the cause along. Prohibition and Gospel Temperance work are well provided for; also many good Campaign Songs are herein found. Our chief desire and aim, however, has been to secure a good selection of enjoyable and enthusing temperance music, suited to the wants of Temperance Organizations and home singing.

We trust that "RALLYING SONGS" will be found both suggestive and inspiring, and much good will result from their use.

PUBLISHER.

TEMPERANCE RALLYING SONGS.

Vote as you Pray.

Priscilla J. Owens.   Asa Hull.

1. Gather and band for the right, Strengthen us, Lord, with Thy might;
E - vil still grows with delay, Christians should vote as they pray.

2. Wine is the curse of the soul, Bitter the dregs of the bowl,
See! they are glowing and red, Tinged with the blood they have shed.

Chorus.
Vote! vote! vote.......... as you pray!..........
Christians should vote as they pray, as they pray,
E - vil still grows with de-lay, Christians should vote as they pray.

3 Vote! let your actions attest
Care for the ones you love best;
Vote! while a thought of your home
Strengthens your heart to o'ercome.

4 Tempted, yield not to despair;
Vote with a hope and a prayer;
Parties for once must give way,
Christians should vote as they pray.

COPYRIGHT, 1887, BY ASA HULL.

Victory at Last.

Lanta Wilson Smith. — Asa Hull.

1. The bat-tle-cry is sound-ing That tells a foe is near;
A foe that brings de-struc-tion On all the heart holds dear.
From moth-ers, wives and chil-dren A cry of sor-row comes:
Re-claim the wand'ring lov'd ones, O save our stricken homes.

2. With shoulder touching shoulder Press on-ward in the fray;
And shrink not in the con-flict Tho' dan-gers mark the way.
God bless the temp'rance ar-my, God speed the cause of right,
God send us men of cour-age, Of wis-dom, truth, and might!

Chorus.

Then rouse, ye men of val-or, Be stead-fast, firm and true;

What are You Sowing.

Rev. E. A. Hoffman.   J. H. Tenney.

3. Are you sowing the seeds that will blossom
    In golden and beautiful grain?
    Or planting but thorns and but thistles,
    To gather but thistles again?

4. Are you sowing to reap in the future
    The Christian's eternal reward?
    Or but to be banished forever
    From Jesus, your glorified Lord?

Saloons Must Go.

EDGAR PAGE.
ASA HULL.
Moderato.

1. The pro-hi-bi-tion host have come, And they have come to stay;
'Tis ter-ror to the friends of rum, We're gaining ev-ery day...
2. We hear the sound the land around, O'er mountain, dell, and plain;
They're coming, and the woods are full, From Texas un-to Maine.

Chorus—a little faster.

They're marching in, just hear the din, What is it all a-bout?
They're say-ing so sa-loons must go, The pro-hi-bi-tion shout!
Saloons must go!... Saloons must go!... SALOONS MUST GO!
must go! must go! must go!

3.
From California's sunny clime,
  Along Atlantic's coast,
'Tis wonder how they grow so fast,
  The prohibition host!

4.
"Fall in, fall in," we're bound to win,
  We'll gather for the right;
For honest men, and men of steel,
  Are wanted for the fight!

4 For "boodle" we are not at work,
  For office or position,
But we are putting in our best
  For *legal* Prohibition.

5 And, brother, we are bound to win,
  Just heed the kind monition;
Come up, and give your autograph
  For Right and Prohibition.

The Danger Signal.

PRISCILLA J. OWENS. G. FROELICH.

1. Stop! stop the train! I see a-head The dan-ger-sig-nal shine,
And where that light is gleaming red, There's trouble on the line.

2. O pause, young man, I see a-head The bar-room windows glow,
And where that light is gleaming red, Death and de-struction show.

Chorus.

Put down the brakes! the warning heed; Remember, friend and stranger,
That all a-long the rail-road line The red light sig-nals dan-ger.

O turn thy steps, the warning heed; Remember, friend and stranger,
That where the bar-room windows shine, Their red light signals danger.

3 O may it warn thee not in vain;
 Alas! that crimson light
Has glanced on many a bloody stain,
 Wild wrath and deadly fight.
  Chorus—O turn thy steps, etc.

4 Then stop the train in time, turn back—
 The warning signal heed—
Before thy home is all a wreck,
 Before thy heart shall bleed.
  Chorus—O turn thy steps, etc.

Rescue the Erring.

Rev. E. A. Hoffman.   *J. H. Tenney.*

1. What can we do for the lost and the per-ish-ing, Go-ing, a-las! without hope to the grave? We can but pray for them, weep o'er them, plead with them, Tell them that Je-sus is might-y to save.
2. What can we do for the souls that are slighting Him, Counting unholy the blood that He gave? We can but fol-low, and gen-tly en-treating them, Point them to Je-sus, the might-y to save.
3. What can we do for the troubled and sorrowing, And for the heart-broken chil-dren of men? We can but pity them, love them, and comfort them, Lead them to Christ, the Re-deemer, a-gain.

Chorus.

Rescue them, rescue them, rescue the erring ones, Bring them to Jesus, and He will re-ceive; Rescue them, rescue them, rescue the fallen ones, Bring them to Jesus, and He will forgive.

COPYRIGHT, 1888, BY ASA HULL.

On to Meet the Foe. 15

Words and Music arranged by Asa Hull.

1. On, brothers, on, to meet the foe that we ab-hor! Rise and put your ar-mor on, and hast-en to the war; Nev-er dare to think that your fighting days are o'er, Un-til the bat-tle's won.
2. On to the res-cue now be-fore it is too late; Let us save a com-rade from so ter-ri-ble a fate; Death may be His por-tion, if we the mor-row wait; So fill the ranks to-day.
3. Strike for the homes where peace does never enter in; Strike for the man-y souls that you may help to win; Strike for love of right, and a-gainst the pow'r of sin, And God shall nerve the arm.

Chorus.

Glo-ry, glo-ry hal-le-lu-jah! Glo-ry hal-le-hal-le-lu-jah! Glo-ry, glo-ry hal-le-lu-jah! Our cause is marching on.

16. Beacon Lights are Shining.

ELIZA M. SHERMAN. S. J. VAIL.

1. Starting from the cra-dle t'ward the grave be-low, Treading in the foot-prints made so long a-go; Do we note the land-marks all a-long the way? Do we stop to gath-er wisdom day by day?
2. Let us learn by oth-ers, shape our lives a-right; O-pen wide our win-dows, let-ting in the light; Im-i-tate the no-ble, cop-y, too, the brave, From our beacon tow-er send a light to save.
3. Note the rock where many stumbled in the night, Trusting not the bea-con, heeding not its light; Ev-er to the watch-tow'r turn a watchful eye, Thou shalt gather wisdom as the days go by.

Chorus.

Bea-con lights are shining from the hills and tow'rs, An-gel voic-es call-ing in the dark-est hours! Let us heed the warn-ing,

COPYRIGHT, 1883, BY ASA HULL.

The Loyal Legion.

Rev. J. Mervin Hull.

1. We are marching onward cheerful and strong, We are fight-ing to de-stroy mighty wrong; We shall conquer, too, tho' long be the fight, For we trust in God, He helps the right.
2. Now the cup of death ex-ults in its reign, Untold thousands like a fiend it has slain; But when loy-al hearts re-spond to the call, Soon its cru-el throne shall sure-ly fall.
3. Raise the standard, then, in East and in West, For our righteous cause let each do his best; "On to vic-to-ry!" our watchword shall be Till our na-tion from the curse is free.

Chorus.

On-ward, for-ward, strong in the right, Lift the ban-ner ho-ly and bright; On to vic-to-ry! cheerful and strong Rings the watch-word as we march along!

COPYRIGHT, 1888, BY ASA HULL.

Prohibition. What is It?

Rev. Charles W. Dennison. Asa Hull.

1. You see I'm a thorough temp'rance man; The crimes and woes of the world I scan, I pity its hard condition;... The fountains of wrong I'd forever dry, To stop the flow I would stop the supply— And *this* is prohibition.....

2. If I knew a baker so badly bold, That in ev'ry loaf of bread he sold, Was arsenical glutition;... I'd oven him up with an iron door, Where he would peddle out death no more—And *this* is prohibition.....

3. If a butcher I saw in the market street, Who murdered the people with putrid meat, The infamous son of perdition!... I'd *stall* him where his stand would be sure, His bread all plain, and his water pure—And *this* is prohibition.....

COPYRIGHT, 1887, BY ASA HULL.

Home, Sweet Home.

JOHN HOWARD PAYNE. — German Melody.

1. 'Mid pleasures and palaces tho' we may roam,
Be it ev-er so humble, there's no place like home;
A charm from the skies seems to hallow us there,
Which, seek thro' the world, is ne'er met with elsewhere.
Home, home, sweet, sweet home! Be it ever so humble, there's no place like home. (Use small note 2d time.)

2 An exile from home, splendor dazzles in vain;
Oh! give me my lowly thatched cottage again;
The birds singing gaily that came at my call,—
Give me them, with the peace of mind, dearer than all.

3 I gaze on the moon, as I trace the drear wild,
And feel that my parents now think of their child:
They look on that moon from their own cottage door,
Through woodbines whose fragrance shall cheer me no more.

Prohibition—Concluded.

4 If I heard a serpent, hid in the grass,
Who stung ev'ry traveler certain to pass,
  I'd curb his infernal ambition;
An iron heel on his head I'd bring,
I'd crush out his life with its poisonous sting—
  And *this* is prohibition.

5 If I had a fold where a wolf crept in,
And ate up the sheep and lambs like sin,
  I'd hold him in tight condition;
I'd stop his howl by choking his breath,
And save my flock by his instant death—
  And *this* is prohibition.

6 If I met a dog that was wont to bite,
Who worried my neighbors day and night,
  I'd fix him by demolition;
In spite of his waggings, his yelpings and tears,
I'd cut off his tail just back of his ears—
  And *this* is prohibition.

Wave the Temperance Banner.

King Al-co-hol shall nev-er stand—We'll conquer by-and-by;

King Al-co-hol shall nev-er stand—We'll conquer by-and-by!

God Speed the Right.

W. E. HICKSON. Music from the German.

1. Now to heav'n our pray'rs ascending, God speed the right; In a noble cause contending, God speed the right; Be our zeal in heav'n recorded, With success on earth rewarded, God speed the right, God speed the right.

2. Be that pray'r a-gain repeat-ed, God speed the right; Ne'er despairing tho' de-feated, God speed the right; Like the good and great in story, If we fail, we fail with glory, God speed the right, God speed the right.

3 Patient, firm, and persevering,
  God speed the right;
Ne'er th' event nor danger fearing,
  God speed the right;
Pains, nor toils, nor trials heeding,
And in heav'ns own time succeeding.
  ‖: God speed the right. :‖

4 Still our onward course pursuing,
  God speed the right;
Ev'ry foe at length subduing,
  God speed the right;
Truth our cause, whate'er delay it,
There's no power on earth can stay it,
  ‖: God speed the right. :‖

Sign the Pledge To-day.

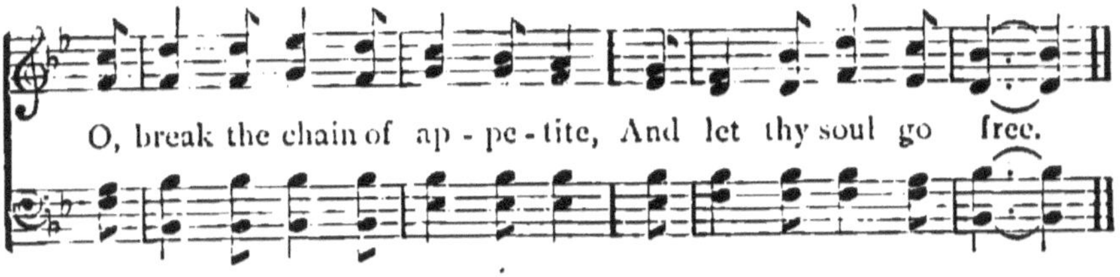

O, break the chain of ap-pe-tite, And let thy soul go free.

Sound the Battle-Cry.

From "Bugle Notes," by permission.   Words and Music by WM. F. SHERWIN.

1. Sound the battle-cry! See! the foe is nigh; Raise the standard high For the Lord;
2. Strong to meet the foe, Marching on we go, While our cause we know Must prevail;
3. Oh! Thou God of all, Hear us when we call; Help us one and all By Thy grace;

Gird your armor on; Stand firm ev'ry one; Rest your cause upon His holy word.
Shield and banner bright, Gleaming in the light; Battling for the right We ne'er can fail.
When the battle's done, And the vict'ry won, May we wear the crown Before Thy face.

Chorus.

Rouse, then, freemen, come from hill and valley; Fathers, brothers, earnest, brave and strong?

Onward, forward, all united, rally, "Death to Alcohol," your battle-song.

Our Ship of State.

G. W. Arbuckle.   Asa Hull.

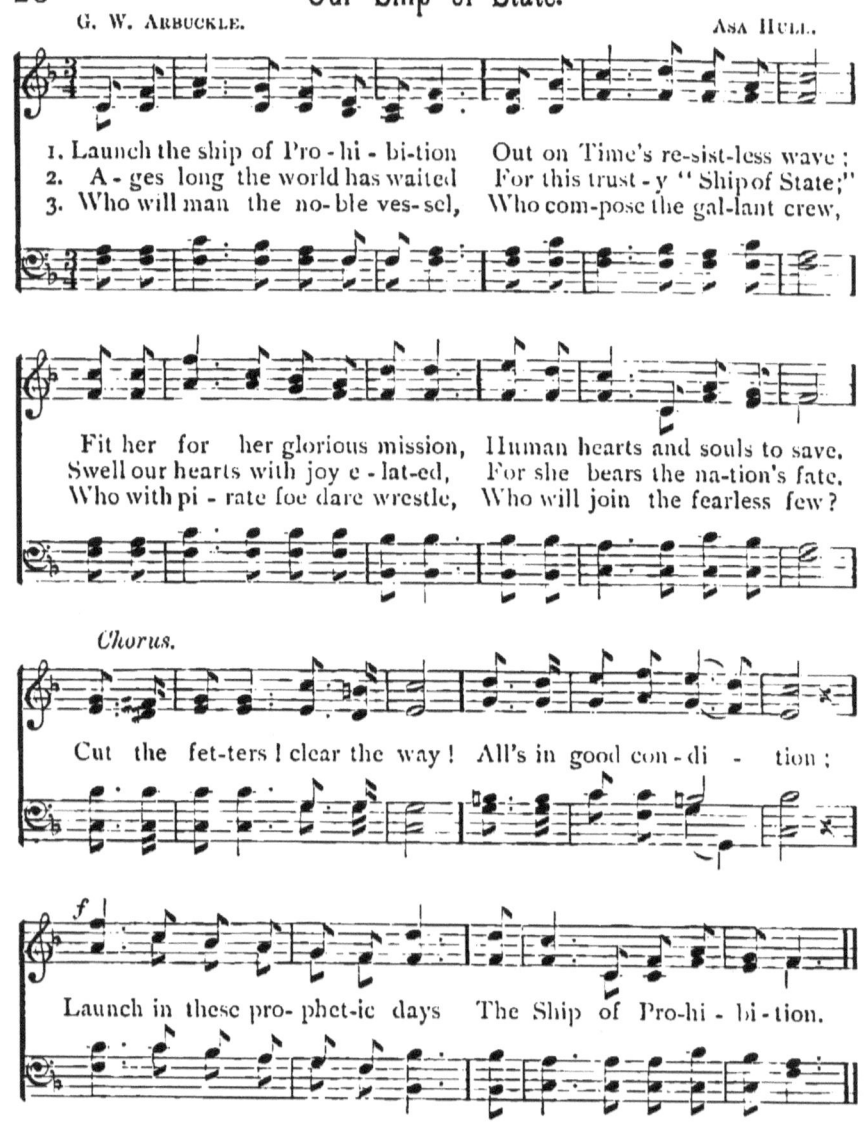

1. Launch the ship of Pro-hi-bi-tion / Out on Time's re-sist-less wave;
2. A-ges long the world has waited / For this trust-y "Ship of State;"
3. Who will man the no-ble ves-sel, / Who com-pose the gal-lant crew,

Fit her for her glorious mission, Human hearts and souls to save.
Swell our hearts with joy e-lat-ed, For she bears the na-tion's fate.
Who with pi-rate foe dare wrestle, Who will join the fearless few?

Chorus.

Cut the fet-ters! clear the way! All's in good con-di-tion;

Launch in these pro-phet-ic days The Ship of Pro-hi-bi-tion.

4 Chartered by the King of Heaven,
   God Himself shall bear her through;
'Mid dark storms she may be driven,
   He can still the tempest, too.

5 Prohibition, then, we name her,
   As we boldly launch her forth;
Licensed wrong shall never shame her,
   Shipwrecked souls will feel her worth.

COPYRIGHT, 1888, BY ASA HULL.

Ye Brave Men, to the Rescue!

Rev. E. A. Hoffman. J. H. Tenney.

1. How man-y, man-y thousands Go down the way of sin!
   A-rouse, ye friends of Je-sus, And bring these lost ones in!
   Are they not all our brothers, The chil-dren of one Lord?
   Go, Christians, to re-claim them; It is your Mas-ter's word.

2. In ev-'ry town and cit-y, In ev-'ry hut and home,
   Throughout the lands and countries, Where hu-man footsteps roam,
   There stalks a gi-ant e-vil De-spoil-ing what is fair,
   That calls for men of pur-pose, Of ear-nest toil and prayer.

3. Oh! help to break the shackels, That make a man a slave!
   Oh! hast-en to the res-cue The fal-len ones to save!
   The God of Heav'n is call-ing To all to take a stand,
   And in the fight with e-vil To lend a help-ing hand.

Chorus.

Ye brave men, to the res-cue! The per-ish-ing re-claim!

Copyright, 1888, by Asa Hull.

3 Not on thine own strength, O my brother, rely,
   That surely would bring thy fall;
   The Lord is thy strength, and in Him shalt thou find
   The help to yet conquer all.

4 We'll give thee our aid in thy pledge to abstain,
   As brothers we'll stand by thee;
   And angels in heav'n will rejoice when they know
   Thy strife and thy victory!

COPYRIGHT, 1888, BY ASA HULL.

34. Keep your Record Clean.

Mrs. A. L. Davison.   Asa Hull.

1. The world's a field of bat-tle, An earnest, noble strife,
2. Great dangers throng about you, The foe is ev-ery-where,
3. From birth to day of dy-ing, Each page is white and fair;

A-gainst a host of e-vils That seek to ru-in life.
Be pure and brave in liv-ing, Be strong to do and dare.
O keep from blot or blemish The sto-ry writ-ten there.

From in-fan-cy to man-hood, The years that lie be-tween,
Touch not the thing un-ho-ly, That will your life de-mean,
In all our earth-ly tri-als No grand-er thing is seen

Are full of sore temp-ta-tion;— O keep your rec-ord clean.
In sta-tion high or low-ly— O keep your rec-ord clean.
Than stain-less, up-right manhood;— O keep your rec-ord clean.

Chorus.

O keep your rec-ord clean, A stain-less page each day;

COPYRIGHT, 1888, BY ASA HULL.

Keep your Record Clean.

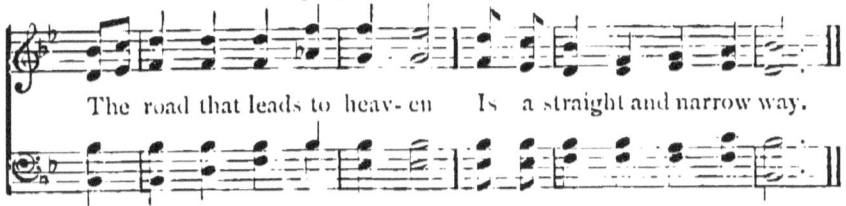

The road that leads to heav-en Is a straight and narrow way.

Ring out the Notes of Warning.

Mrs. E. W. Chapman.   J. H. Tenney.
Con espressione.

1. Lost to a sense of du-ty, Wreck of a no-ble frame,
2. Shorn of his for-mer greatness, Robbed of his gen-'rous heart,
3. Down in the gut-ter ly-ing, Less than a beast he knows;

Gone in his pris-tine beau-ty, Tarnished his wor-thy name.
Lost his Cre-a-tor's like-ness, Wounded in ev-'ry part.
Low in the darkness dy-ing, Sad in his last re-pose.

Chorus.

Ring out the notes of warning, Ring, ere it be too late; Those who have

ad lib.

not yet fall-en Save from a drunkard's fate, Save from a drunkard's fate.

COPYRIGHT, 1888, BY ASA HULL.

Keep out of the Gutter.

Mrs. E. W. Chapman.   Male Voices.   Chas. Edw. Prior.

1. The storm-cloud is dark, and the air is snow-filled, And fearful the breezes that mutter; But, lo! as we pass is a form that is chilled, The form of a man in the gutter.

2. He once was a sage whom the world could esteem, And wise were the words he could utter; But now like a man in a pitiful dream, Degraded he lies in the gutter.

Chorus—Faster.

Come, boys, and sign; yes, sign the pledge to-night, And then keep the promise you utter; Your names on the pledge if you place right away, You'll never be found in the gutter.

3. Alas! for the wine which in private he drank,
Concealed by the close-fitting shutter,
He low in the depths of depravity sank,
At last to be found in the gutter.

4. Oh, who can the evils of drinking portray,
The sorrow and grief who can utter;
A tithe of the heartache of kindred convey,
Of him who is found in the gutter.

Copyright, 1888, by Asa Hull.

Awake, Columbia, Awake.

3 No minions from a foreign land—*strange land*
  Before Americans shall stand,
  To trample down our Sabbath day,—*our day*,
  Or cast our Bible yet away.—*away*.

4 Let Prohibition be our cry,—*our cry*,
  For Prohibition let us vie,
  And let each loyal freeman stand—*now stand*
  For " God and home and native land."—*our land*.

COPYRIGHT, 1888, BY ASA HULL.

The Light from Home.

LANTA WILSON SMITH.   Male Voices.   ASA HULL.

1. A fish-er-boy went sail-ing out, The wind was fresh and fair,
2. The morn was fair, but ere the night A storm came o'er the sea,
3. Then like a tin-y star appeared A far-off, fee-ble light,

He bounded o'er the wa-ters blue With-out a thought of care.
And thro' the chill-ing, blind-ing mist He drift-ed help-less-ly.
It's stead-y, cheering, sav-ing beam Had pierced the gloomy night.

As sights a-long the shore grew dim, One lit-tle speck a-far—
The breakers roared, the darkness fell, The boy was filled with fear;
"'Tis mother's light!" he cried with joy, "I'll steer by moth-er's light,

His moth-er's cot-tage on the cliff—Was like a guid-ing star!
No light, no voice, no arm to save, He felt that death was near.
'Twill guide me safe-ly to the shore—She's saved her boy to-night!"

4.
Your boy sails out in life to-day,
   There's many a storm to meet;
And when the darkness settles down,
   And wild waves round him beat,
Have you the pow'r to guide him safe,
   Through sin's bewildering night?
Can he shout gladly thro' the storm—
   "I'll steer by mother's light?"

5.
O mother, hold your lamp aloft!
   A word, a smile, a prayer,
That lights the mem'ry of your child,
   May save from many a snare.
Then trim, with never-failing faith,
   Your lamps of truth and right;
So 'twill be safe, thro' life or death,
   To steer by mother's light.

COPYRIGHT, 1888, BY ASA HULL.

4.
Your boy sails out in life to-day,
  There's many a storm to meet;
And when the darkness settles down,
  And wild waves round him beat,
Have you the pow'r to guide him safe,
  Through sin's bewildering night?
Can he shout gladly thro' the storm—
  "I'll steer by mother's light?"

5.
O mother, hold your lamp aloft!
  A word, a smile, a prayer,
That lights the mem'ry of your child,
  May save from many a snare.
Then trim, with never-failing faith,
  Your lamps of truth and right;
So 'twill be safe, thro' life or death,
  To steer by mother's light.

Break the Chain.

cho-rus shall be, In the name of our God, the in - e - bri-ate is free!

Vote as you Pray.

PRISCILLA J. OWENS.   Male Voices.   ASA HULL.

1. Gather and band for the right, Strengthen us, Lord, with Thy might;
2. Wine is the curse of the soul, Bit-ter the dregs of the bowl,

E - vil still grows with de-lay, Christians should vote as they pray.
See! they are glowing and red, Tinged with the blood they have shed.

Chorus.

Vote! vote! vote....... as you pray!
Christians should vote as they pray, as they pray!

E - vil still grows with de-lay, Christians should vote as they pray.

3 Vote! let your actions attest
Care for the ones you love best:
Vote! while a thought of your home
Strengthens your heart to o'ercome.

4 Tempted, yield not to despair;
Vote with a hope and a prayer:
Parties for once must give way,
Christians should vote as they pray.

COPYRIGHT, 1887, BY ASA HULL.

3 Then let the ballots rattle,
   Don't you hear, don't you hear?
   Come push along the battle,
   Don't you hear?

4 There comes a mighty wonder,
   Don't you know, don't you know?
   Saloons must all go under,
   Don't you know?

I may not be a Prophet.

46
G. S. W.
GEORGE S. WEEKS.

1. I may not be a prophet, But I think I hear the song
2. I may not be a prophet, But I think that I shall see
3. I may not be a prophet, But I think that I shall hear

Of chil-dren in their hap-py homes, The mighty strain prolong—
The reel-ing drunkard live no more In ab-ject slav-e-ry!
In lov-ing homes no more the curse Of drunkards smite the ear;

That whiskey-shops, in ev-'ry street, Have closed no more to sell
No rum-sell-er shall then grow rich Up-on the souls of men,
The orphan'd child and tor-tur'd wife Shall cry no more to God;

The liq-uid fire that drags the souls Of pa-rents down to hell!
Nor lure the vic-tims of their power With-in their wolf-ish den!
For He shall smite the De-mon Rum With His a-veng-ing rod!

Chorus.

I may not be a prophet, But I think I hear the song

COPYRIGHT, 1888, BY ASA HULL.

I may not be a Prophet.

Of Pro-hi-bi-tion thro' the world, Ech-oed the years a-long!

4 I may not be a prophet,
  But methinks I hear a voice
That bids the suffering ones of earth
  To rise and to rejoice !
The tidal wave of Christian love,
  Of peace and kindliness,
Is sweeping on beneath God's sky,
  His children all to bless.

5 I may not be a prophet,
  But the glorious day's at hand,
When Rum and Crime shall walk no more
  Red-handed through this land !
When Murder, with its dreadful shriek,
  Shall pierce no more the night,
But love shall rule the human heart
  With Truth and Joy and Right !

On the Field of Battle.

Rev. E. H Nevin, D.D.

With Energy.

1. Live on the field of bat-tle ! Be earn-est in the fight;
2. Watch on the field of bat-tle ! The foe is ev-'ry-where,

Stand forth with man-ly courage, And strug-gle for the right.
His fie-ry darts fly thickly, Like light-ning thro' the air.

Live, live, live ! Live on the field of bat-tle.
Watch, watch, watch ! Watch on the field of bat-tle.

3 Pray on the field of battle !
  God works with those who pray ;
His mighty arm can nerve us,
  And make us win the day.
    Pray, pray, pray !
  Pray on the field of battle.

4 Die on the field of battle !
  'Tis noble thus to die ;
God smiles on valiant soldiers,—
  Their record is on high.
    Die, die, die !
  Die on the field of battle.

Shun all Liquid Fire.

Rev. George M. Preston. Asa Hull.

1. Look not up-on the foaming beer, Nor ci-der's sparkling flow,
2. Look not up-on the reddened wine, That "Moves itself a-right;"

For they will lead to sor-rows here, And then to depths of woe.
Their tott'ring steps to death in-cline, Who view its col-or bright.

Chorus.

But on cold wa-ter's smiling flood Re-new your constant gaze;

For that will do you on-ly good, And give you prosp'rous days.

3 Look not on whiskey's bottled rage,
Nor brandy's fiery flame;
They neither burning thirst assuage,
Nor save a ruined name.

4 Look not on any liquid fire,
That burns upon the lip;
It will his foulest deeds inspire
Who takes the fatal sip.

COPYRIGHT, 1880, BY ASA HULL.

We'll Conquer or Die.

3 Strike deep and unerring, nor dare to retreat,
  Though thousands by thousands the enemy meet;
  The thicker the foemen, the firmer stand by,
  Rememb'ring your watchword, "We conquer, or die."

4 Go forth in the pathway your forefathers trod;
  Ye, too, fight for freedom, your Captain is God!
  Fling out your broad banners against the blue sky,
  And shout, like true soldiers, "We conquer, or die."

5 Not chains for the tyrant, for chains are in vain,
  He's planning already to break them in twain;
  But raise your deep voices, and shout the war-cry:
  Death! death for the tyrant, "We conquer, or die."

Cheer up, You'll Win the Day.

ASA HULL.

1. Cheer up! cheer up! desponding ones, And let the past go by;
It beck-ons to each wav'ring soul To look a-head with cheer;
For in the fut-ure gleams a star, Whose radiance lights the sky,
For he who tru-ly seeks for good, Will find it ev-er near.

Chorus.
Cheer up!.... cheer up!.... and let the past go by;
For in the fut-ure gleams a star, Whose radiance lights the sky.

2.
Cheer up! cheer up! and in the strife
  Against the curse contend;
For soberness and goodly deeds
  Will soon secure a friend.
The heart that struggles long and hard,
  And wins the day at last,
Can boast of more than he who glides
  More smoothly evils past.

3.
Cheer up! cheer up! you'll win the day,
  If faithfully you try;
There's no device can keep you back,
  If *will* says, " never die."
The race is for the diligent,
  The prize is ever sure
To those while pressing firmly on,
  Unto the end endure.

Yield not to Temptation.

H. R. PALMER, Mus. Doc.

1. Yield not to temp-ta-tion, For yielding is sin; Each vic-t'ry will
2. Shun e-vil com-panions, Bad language dis-dain, God's name hold in
3. To him that o'ercom-eth God giv-eth a crown; Thro' faith we shall

help you Some oth-er to win; Fight manful-ly on-ward,
rev-'rence, Nor take it in vain; Be thoughtful and ear-nest,
con-quer, Tho' oft-en cast down; He who is our Sav-iour,

Dark passions sub-due, Look ever to Je-sus, He'll carry you through.
Kind-hearted and true, Look ever to Je-sus, He'll carry you through.
Our strength will renew, Look ever to Je-sus, He'll carry you through.

Chorus.

Ask the Sav-iour to help you, Com-fort, strengthen, and keep you;

He is will-ing to aid you, He will car-ry you through.

58. In God we Trust.

MARY D. JAMES.   ASA HULL.

1. Come, join our Temp'rance Band, Come, rally for the right; And war a-gainst the cru-el foe That caused our na-tion's blight.
2. Come, join our ranks to-day,.. We go at Heaven's command To ban-ish the de-stroyer, Rum, The curse of our fair land.

Chorus.
Then gird the ar-mor on, The de-mon Rum as-sail; While Is-rael's God is on our side, Our cause can nev-er fail.

3 In God omnipotent
   We firmly place our trust,
  Who nerved young David's arm to strike
   The Giant in the dust.

4 God's army is defied,
   By this gigantic foe,
  But He will give His people strength
   To lay the monster low.

5 Our Banner is unfurled,
   Its glorious motto see!
  "In God we trust"—in Isreal's God,
   "Who giveth victory."

6 Then forward let us move,—
   To certain conquest go,—
  The *mighty God* our Leader is,
   We're sure to crush the foe.

COPYRIGHT, 1877, BY ASA HULL.

60. The Writing on the Wall.

MARIAN FROELICH.   Male Voices.   G. FROELICH.

1. King Al-co-hol sat at his roy-al spread-board, Like haughty Belshazzar of old, And loud were the cheers from his rev-el-ing horde, As they drank from their beakers of gold; Well guarded was he by his courtier-like train, Destruction and Ru-in and Woe, And high rang their clam-or-ous cho-rus a-gain, Con-fu-sion to Temp'rance, our foe.

2. King Al-co-hol nod-ded, ap-prov-ing his head, And drank with a will to their toast; And then with a look full of cun-ning, he said, My power is no i-dle boast; And yet there's an en-e-my threatens my reign, Its strength it is great, I al-lege, Un-less we op-pose 'twill as-cen-den-cy gain, This foe is the Temperance pledge.

3. De-stroy it, de-stroy it, the mad-den-ing cry, That shouted the wine-heated band, We'll shat-ter its pow-er, and Temp'rance must die, King Al-co-hol rul-eth the land; This pledge is the badge of the good and the true, Freemen it would make of our slaves; O'er ru-ins 'twould build up fair structure a-new, 'Twould rob even Death of his graves.

COPYRIGHT, 1888, BY ASA HULL.

The Temperance Call.

Allegro con fuoco. — FRANZ ABT.

1. Hear the Temp'rance call, Freemen, one and all! Hear your country's earnest cry;
2. Leave the shop and farm, leave your bright hearths warm; To the polls! the land to save;
3. Hail our fatherland! Here thy children stand, All resolved, u-nit-ed, true,

See your native land Lift its beck'ning hand, Sons of freedom, come ye nigh.
Let your leaders be True and noble, free, Fearless, temp'rate, true and brave.
In the Temp'rance cause, Ne'er to faint or pause! This our purpose is, and vow.

Chorus.

Chase the monster from our shore, Let his cru-el reign be o'er;
Chase the monster from our shore, Let his cru-el reign be o'er.

The Writing on the Wall—Concluded.

4 King Alcohol shuddered; for, lo! on the wall,
   In letters of fire, his doom;
And silence o'erspreadeth the banquetting hall,
   The revel is ended in gloom.
A hand traces slowly, in letters of flame,
   Thy rule, O Iniquity, ends!
And Temp'rance thy far-reaching empire will claim,
   While peace and prosperity blends.

The Day is Breaking.

Marian Froelich. G. Froelich.

With Energy.

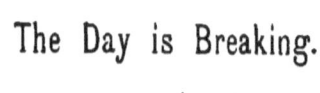

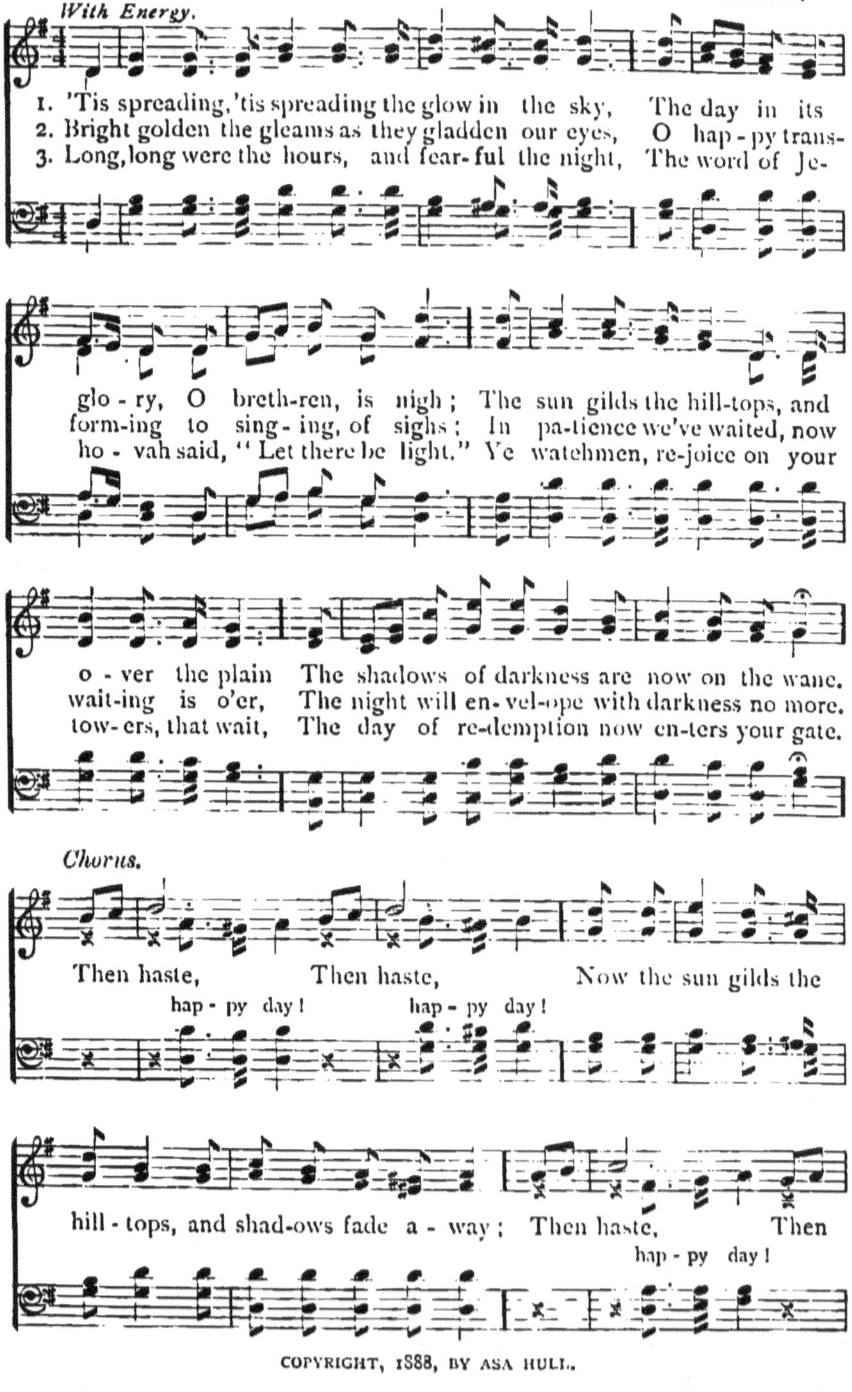

The Cross and Banner.

3 But opposed in rank unbroken,
 Men of God, contest the field ;
Have they not the sign and token,
 Wrong to right must ever yield ?

4 Courage, soldier, be undaunted,
 God and Temp'rance be your boast;
Vain the strength your foes have vaunted,
 On your side the " Lord of host."

# The Temperance Warfare.

gain and a-gain, The King shall be vanquished, his al-lies be slain.

Greeting Refrain.

Scherzando.

1. Oh, list the song we sing to-night, And welcome it with smiles so bright;
2. We do our best, kind friends, to-night, And greet you with our music light;
3. Our music soft shall weave a spell, En-chanting as a distant bell,

Our kindly greeting don't disdain, But list-en to our glad re-frain.
Now cheer us on our hap-py way, And list-en to our mer-ry lay.
As far o'er hill and dell it floats, Enchanting as the sweet birds' notes.

Solo.

La la la......
La la la la la la la la la la la la la la,

La la la......
La la la la la la la la la la la la la la.

3.
Wives and sisters ask with sorrow,
  Will you take the social glass?
Let this cheering promise follow,
  "We'll not take the social glass."

4.
Youth and beauty may entice you,
  Now to take the social glass;
O, resist the fatal challenge,
  Never take the social glass.

COPYRIGHT, 1888, BY ASA HULL.

Push the Cause Along.

The Jubilee of Temperance.

KEY OF A♭. TUNE—"Battle-Cry of Freedom."

1 WE have met you here again, friends, to sing you our refrain,
   Shouting the Jubilee of Temp'rance ;
  We will join in song together, and this shall be our strain,
   Shouting the Jubilee of Temp'rance.

CHORUS.—Temp'rance forever, hurrah, friends, hurrah !
   Keep from the rum-shop forever and far ;
  And we'll rally round the Pledge, friends, united in our cause,
   Shouting the Jubilee of Temp'rance.

2 We have signed the good old Pledge, that our brothers signed before,
   Shouting the Jubilee of Temp'rance ;
  And will number in our ranks a million signers more,
   Shouting the Jubilee of Temp'rance.

3 We are springing to the call, the young, the old, and all,
   Shouting the Jubilee of Temp'rance ;
  And we'll banish alcohol from the parlor, shop, and hall,
   Shouting the Jubilee of Temp'rance.

4 We will raise the fallen up, and will make them sober men,
   Shouting the Jubilee of Temp'rance ;
  Till the hills and valleys ring, this Temp'rance song we'll sing,
   Shouting the Jubilee of Temp'rance.

Rally Round our Banner.

For the hour of mighty conflict With the rum-fiend draweth nigh.

4 Then, in mighty, fearless conflict,
  We will grapple with the foe;
  Where he plants his hated colors,
  There our cherished flag will go;
  Till at last, in final triumph,
  Heaven's smile shall bid it wave,
  Emblem faithful of redemption,
  O'er the fallen demon's grave.

So will I Comfort Thee.

MARY D. JAMES.   J. W. KIRKPATRICK.

1. So will I comfort thee, Poor sorrowing child of care; Thy heavy
   load of woe, Upon my heart I bear. I know thy pains, and griefs, and fears,
   I hear thy sighs, and count thy tears: So will I comfort, comfort thee.
2. So will I comfort thee, Thro' all life's dreary way; I'll be thy
   constant guide, I'll keep thee night and day; No foes, no perils need'st thou fear,
   For I, thy God, am always near: So will I comfort, comfort thee.

3 So will I comfort thee,
  E'en I, the *mighty God*;
  Unchanging is My love,
  Unfailing is My word.
  No mother's love can equal Mine,
  No arms so strong as arms Divine;
  So will I comfort thee.

4 So will I comfort thee;
  From every stormy blast,
  I'll hide thee with My wings,
  "Till all life's storms are past,"
  Then bear thee to the heavenly shore,
  Where sorrow's tears shall fall no more:
  So will I comfort thee.

COPYRIGHT, 1880, BY ASA HULL.

Ask me not to Sip the Wine.

For, left with-in the gob-let bright, It harm-less-ly may shine.

3.
O, urge me not to drink the wine,
The sparkling ruby wine,
For, though within the goblet bright
It harmlessly may shine,
It holds a flame to wrap the life
In more than midnight gloom,
And sets upon the precious soul
The seal of hopeless doom.

4.
I dare not, will not sip the wine,
The sparkling ruby wine,
For, though within the goblet bright
It harmlessly may shine,
If I should sip the treach'rous draught,
A brother or a friend
Might be thereby induced to drink,
And ruin be the end.

The Voice of Truth.

Special Arrangement.

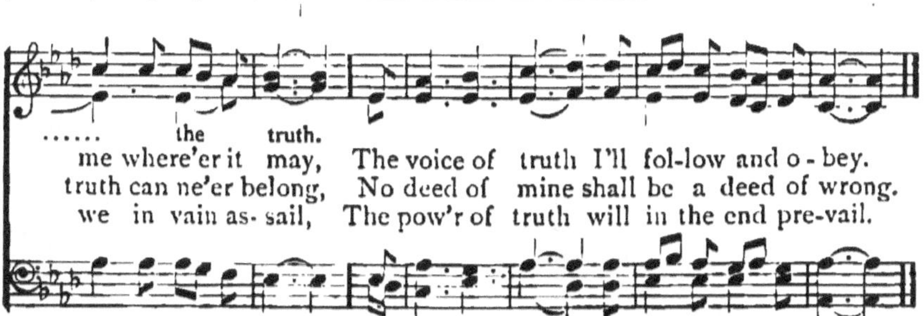

Moderato.

1. My days of youth, tho' not from folly free, I prize the truth, the
2. My foot-steps lead, O truth, and mould my will, In word and deed, my
3. The strength of youth, we see it soon de-cay; But strong is truth, and

Same for each verse. I'll keep..........
more the world I see; I'll keep the straight and narrow path, lead
du-ty to ful-fil; Dis-hon-est arts and self-ish aims to
stron-ger ev-ery day; Tho' falsehood seem a mighty pow'r, which

...... the truth.
me where'er it may, The voice of truth I'll fol-low and o-bey.
truth can ne'er belong, No deed of mine shall be a deed of wrong.
we in vain as-sail, The pow'r of truth will in the end pre-vail.

Courage, Brother.

The Lord will Provide.

Mrs. M. A. Cook. Prof. C. S. Harrington.

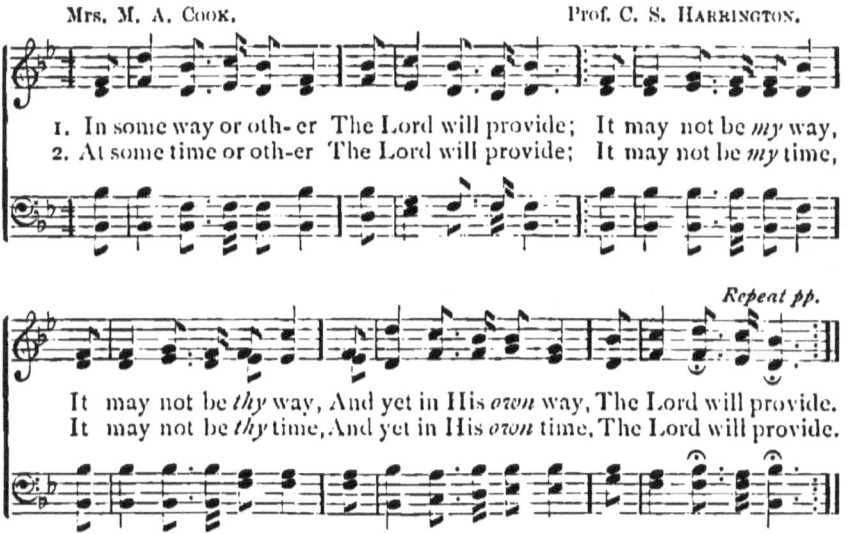

3 Despond, then, no longer;
  The Lord will provide;
  And this be the token—
  No word He hath spoken
  Was ever yet broken,—
    The Lord will provide.
  It may not be *my* way, etc.

4 March on, then, right boldly;
  The sea shall divide;
  The pathway made glorious
  With shoutings victorious,
  We'll join in the chorus,
    The Lord will provide.
  It may not be *my* way, etc.

3.
They cluster all about our path,
  The poor, the lone, the sad ;
An outstretched hand may save from sin,
  A word may make them glad.
No human heart has sunk so low
  But what some good is there,
We may awake the sleeping germ
  By love and tender care.

4.
In helping others we are blest
  And paid an hundredfold,
With knowledge of the Father's smile
  And joy and peace untold.
Thus deeds of kindness, acts of love,
  Bring fruitage rich and rare,
And angels watching from above
  See naught on earth so fair.

COPYRIGHT, 1886, BY ASA HULL.

Be Men of Action.

MARIAN FROELICH. G. FROELICH.

3. Where his poisoned coils are trailing
   Death holds revel wild and high;
   And his music is the wailing
   Of a broken heart's sad cry.

4. 'Tis Intemperance that enfoldeth,
   Killing in its murderous clasp
   All the manhood that it holdeth,
   Ere relaxing its fell grasp.

COPYRIGHT, 1888, BY ASA HULL.

God is Marching On.

JULIA WARD HOWE.   ASA HULL.

1. Mine eyes have seen the glo-ry of the com-ing of the Lord,
2. He hath sounded forth the trumpet that shall nev-er call re-treat;
3. In the beau-ty of the lil - ies Christ was born a-cross the sea,

He is trampling out the vintage where the grapes of wrath are stored;
He is sift-ing out the hearts of men be - fore His judgment-seat;
With a glo - ry in His bo-som that trans-fig-ures you and me;

He hath loosed the fateful lightnings of His ter - ri-ble swift sword,
O, be swift, my soul, to an-swer Him; be ju - bi-lant, my feet!
As He died to make men ho-ly, let us die to make men free,

Chorus.

His truth is marching on! Marching, marching, His truth is
Our God is marching on!
While God is marching on!

marching on! Marching, marching, * His truth is marching on!

* *Close with last line of each verse.*

Mother's Praying for You.

Battle Hymn of the Women's Crusade.

(Music on page 78.)

1. THE light of truth is breaking, on the mountain top it gleams;
   Let it flash along our valleys, let it glitter on our streams,
   Till all our land awakens in its flush of golden beams.
       Our God is marching on.

2. With purpose strong and steady, in the great Jehovah's name,
   We rise to snatch our kindred from the depths of woe and shame;
   And the jubilee of freedom to the slaves of sin proclaim.
       Our God is marching on.

3. Our strength is in Jehovah, and our cause is in His care;
   With almighty arms to help us, we have faith to do and dare,
   While confiding in the promise that the Lord will answer prayer,
       Our God is marching on.

Nothing but Leaves.

85

Moderato. S. J. Vail.

1. Nothing but leaves! The Spirit grieves O'er years of wasted life;
2. Nothing but leaves! No gathered sheaves Of life's fair ripening grain;

O'er sins indulged while conscience slept, O'er vows and prom-is-es un-kept,
We sow our seeds; lo, tares and weeds—Words, *idle* words, for earnest deeds—

And reap from years of strife— Nothing but leaves! Nothing but leaves!
Then reap, with toil and pain, Nothing but leaves! Nothing but leaves!

3.
Nothing but leaves! Sad mem'ry weaves
  No veil to hide the past:
And as we trace our weary way,
And count each lost and misspent day
  We sadly find at last—
    Nothing but leaves!

4.
Ah! who shall thus the Master meet,
  And bring but withered leaves?
Ah! who shall at the Saviour's feet,
Before the awful judgment-seat,
  Lay down for golden sheaves,
    Nothing but leaves?

We will Work on—Concluded.

2 The cries of the suffering, helpless, and poor,
    Bid us work on, bid us work on;
  The victim who enters the rumseller's door
    Will pray for the downfall of rum.
  The mother who prays for her wandering child,
    Bids us work on, bids us work on;
  O list to her pleading, so broken and wild,
    "Come rescue! O rescue my son!"

3 O list to the prayers of the poor, weeping wife,
    Urging us on, urging us on;
  For misery, suffering, anguish, and strife,
    Now dwell in that once happy home.
  The little ones bare-footed, ragged, and cold,
    Bid us work us, bid us work on;
  O come to their rescue, and bravely take hold
    And help us in conquering Rum.

86. Be True to your Manhood.

ELIZA M. SHERMAN. HARRY SANDERS.

Slowly, and with Expression.

1. You are leav-ing the hap-py home-cir-cle to-day For the world with its sor-row and joy, But think of the word that I say to you now, Be true to your manhood, my boy. Be true to your manhood, be true, And here is a mot-to for you; Stand fast, and yield not to tempta-tion and wrong, Be true to your manhood, be true.

2. Look thou not on the wine-cup that glit-ters so red, Go thou not where the bar-ta-pers glow; They but beck-on you on to lure you a-way, These signals of danger and woe.

3. Oh! then shun the broad way, tho' a flow-er-y path, It will end in deep trouble and woe, Trust it not, but in-cline to the old beaten path That your loved ones would have you to go.

Chorus.

COPYRIGHT, 1888, BY ASA HULL.

There's a Ring to our Cheer.

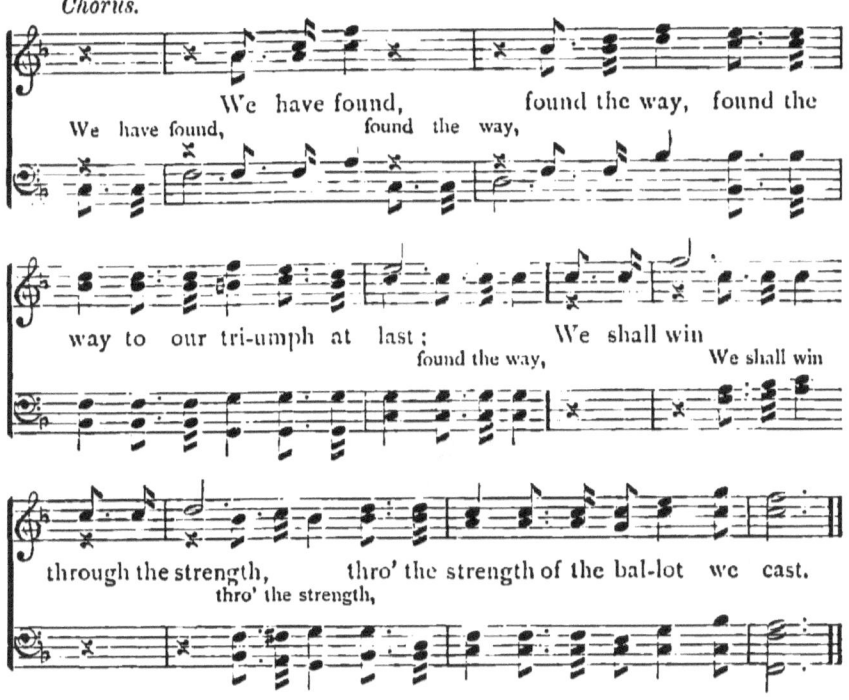

Joyous Tidings.

KEY OF B♭.   TUNE—"Ring the Bells of Heaven."

1 SHOUT the joyous tidings! there's glad news for all!
  Shout! our righteous cause is gaining ground!
  See the millions saved from alcoholic thrall,
  Listen! how their ringing cheers resound!

CHORUS.—Vict'ry! vict'ry! hear the music swell!
  Vict'ry! vict'ry! how the voices dwell!
  'Tis the Temp'rance army, like a mighty sea,
  Pouring forth the rapture of the free.

2 Shout the joyous tidings! there's glad news to-day,
  Wand'rers are returning to the fold;
  Spread the welcome tidings, speed it on the way,
  Rum will soon be neither made nor sold.

3 Shout the glorious tidings! glorious news to-night!
  All the states are wheeling into line;
  Firmly standing on the side of God and right,
  Led and strengthened by a hand divine.

4 Shout the joyous tidings! soldiers everywhere
  From the North and from the South they come;
  Be it East or West, our banner's floating there,
  Bearing the device of "Death to Rum!"

Our Noble Temperance Girls.

Sometimes I long to raise the shout, And vict'ry's flag unfurl,
O girls! tho' dearest friends may tempt, Be steadfast, firm, and true,
To make the path of right so fair, That thousands you may win,

'Tis when I see among the ranks A noble temp'rance girl.
Your strength, and truth, and purity, Will speed the end in view.
From all the deadly snares that lurk In gilded halls of sin.

Refrain.

The temp'rance girls, The temp'rance girls,
God bless the girls,........ God bless the girls,........
Our noble temp'rance girls; God bless the girls, the temp'rance girls,
Our noble temp'rance girls.

4 The pow'r you wield for truth and right,
  None but the Father knows;
  The glorious vict'ries girls have won,
  The heavenly record shows.
  And when at last in heaven's light
  These noble deeds appear,
  I'd like to share the sweet " Well done,"
  Our temp'rance girls will hear.

The Banner of Temperance.

1. Oh! say can you see by the dawn's early light, That intemp'rance, once firm-ly entrenched, is a-wan-ing?
Don't you see that the right yet will triumph o'er might? For the cause that we cher-ish is stead-i-ly gaining;

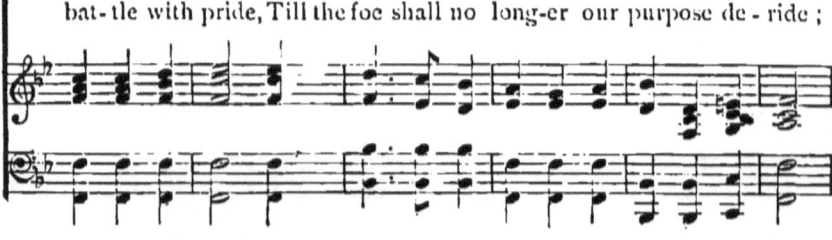

On hu-man-i-ty's side we will bat-tle with pride, Till the foe shall no long-er our purpose de-ride;

The Banner of Temperance.

2 Oh! say don't you see that the time is at hand
  When the power of the rum-fiend shall surely be broken?
There's a spirit abroad, and a force in the land,
  That shall smite the vile monster, his doom hath been spoken.
Then prepare for the fray, bravely battle for aye,
'Till the Demon shall yield, and his minions give way.
And the banner of Temp'rance shall proudly wave
O'er the land of the free, and the home of the brave!

3 Oh! say don't you see that the conflict is nigh,
  Freemen armed with the ballot our nation redeeming?
In martial array see their banners wave high,
  Loyal Temperance voters in myriads are teeming!
They are shouting aglow, that saloons must all go,
With their train of pollution, destruction and woe!
And the banner of Temp'rance shall proudly wave
O'er the land of the free, and the home of the brave!

COPYRIGHT, 1888, BY ASA HULL.

The Wife's Prayer.

3 Ringing above the wild jest and the song,
   He heareth the voice of a prayer;
And the days of his youth to his memory throng,
   With their promise and purposes fair;
And forth from the place of temptation and sin
   He hastes to his own cottage door,
And he joined in the prayer that arose within,
   And the sorrow of years is o'er.

The Happy Days Gone by. 101

Chorus.

Oh! if father would stop his drinking, It would make our hearts so glad;

But now our home is un-hap-py, And always seems so sad.

4 And mother, oh! she looks so sad,
  So wan with grief and care,
  The lines of sorrow mark her face,
  And silvered is her hair;
  Her life has lost its holy charm,
  Her heart knows only tears,
  For father has not cared for her
  For, lo! these many years.

5 When will the days return again
  That were to us so glad?
  When will the hours of sorrow cease,
  The hours that are so sad?
  O Father kind! look down on us
  In pity from Thy throne,
  And give us back our father's love,
  And make his heart Thine own.

Drink is Raging.

ASA HULL.

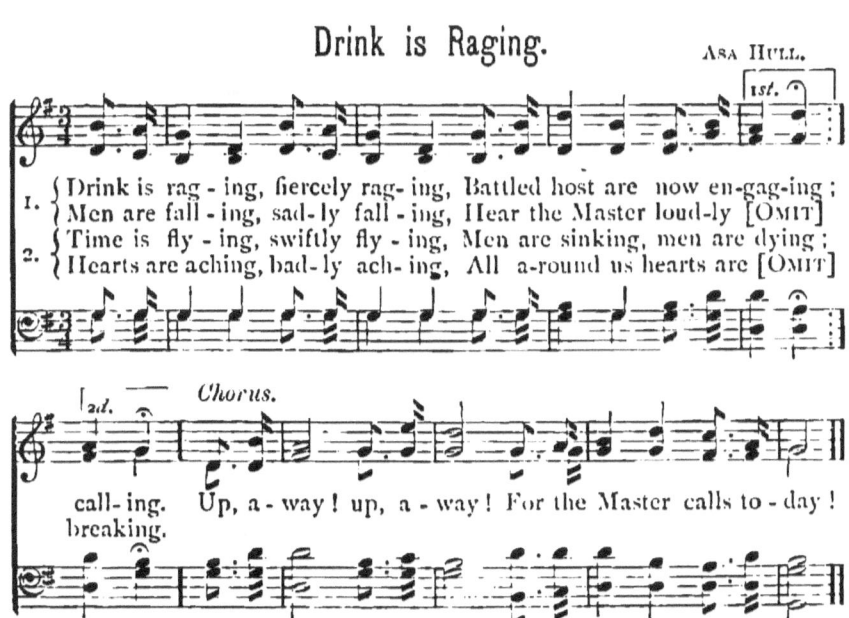

1. { Drink is rag-ing, fiercely rag-ing, Battled host are now en-gag-ing;
    Men are fall-ing, sad-ly fall-ing, Hear the Master loud-ly [OMIT]
2. { Time is fly-ing, swiftly fly-ing, Men are sinking, men are dying;
    Hearts are aching, bad-ly ach-ing, All a-round us hearts are [OMIT]

Chorus.

call-ing. Up, a-way! up, a-way! For the Master calls to-day!
breaking.

Right over Wrong.

3 And all the old distilleries
  Shall perish and burn together,
 The Brandy, Rum, and Gin, and Beer,
  And all such, whatsoever.
 The world begins to feel the fire,
  And e'en the poor besotter,
 To save himself from burning up,
  Jumps in the cooling water.

Papa Darling, do not Leave us.

3 Mamma never heard you harshly
  Speak, to her or us, before,
Angels gathered round her bedside,
  And to heav'n her gently bore.
Papa darling, now you never
  Kiss us as you gently smile,
And you frown on us whenever
  We would talk to you a while.

4 From the eyes the tears that gathered
  Down the bearded cheeks now flow,
Purposes, both pure and holy,
  Love's awakening power show.
Papa's darlings, closely folded,
  Lie within his shelt'ring arms,
And a purer life is moulded,
  Broken are the wine-cup's charms.

Sparkling Fountain.

Sicilian Hymn.

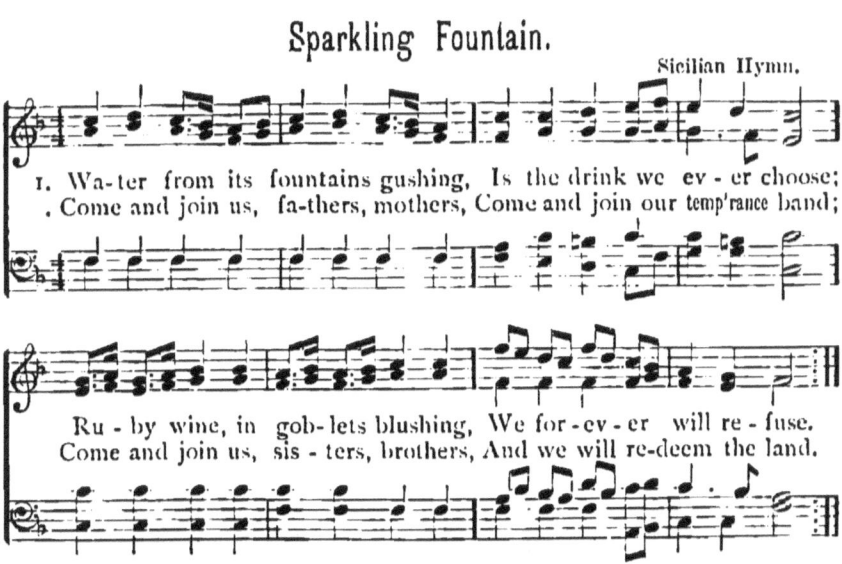

3 Heed, O heed the call of duty,
  In the temp'rance ranks appear;
Hoary age and maiden beauty,
  With the strong and brave are here.

4 Come and drink, with shouts of gladness,
  Water from the gushing spring;
Bid adieu to wine and sadness,
  And with cheerful voices sing.

106. Go in Jesus' Name.

Mrs. E. W. Chapman.
J. H. Tenney.

1. Homes there are of want and sor-row, Where the sunlight ne'er ap-pears;..... On-ly grief, and woe, and pal-lor, 'Mid the flow of burning tears. There no kind-ly word is spok-en, None to tell of Je-sus' love;....

2. There are hearts so sad and wea-ry, Weak, and faint, and sore op-prest,..... Hun-g'ring for the words of com-fort, Long-ing for the boon of rest. There are children lone-ly, cry-ing For a pa-rent's watchful care;....

Copyright, 1888, by Asa Hull.

3 There are fathers, mothers, brothers,
   Bound in chains of sin and shame,
Nothing but the power of Jesus
   Can the guilty hearts reclaim.
Rum hath wrought this woe and ruin,
   Robbed these homes of daily food,
Fettered every noble impulse,
   Every true desire for good.—*Chorus.*

Temperance Marseilles.

Vote for Prohibition.

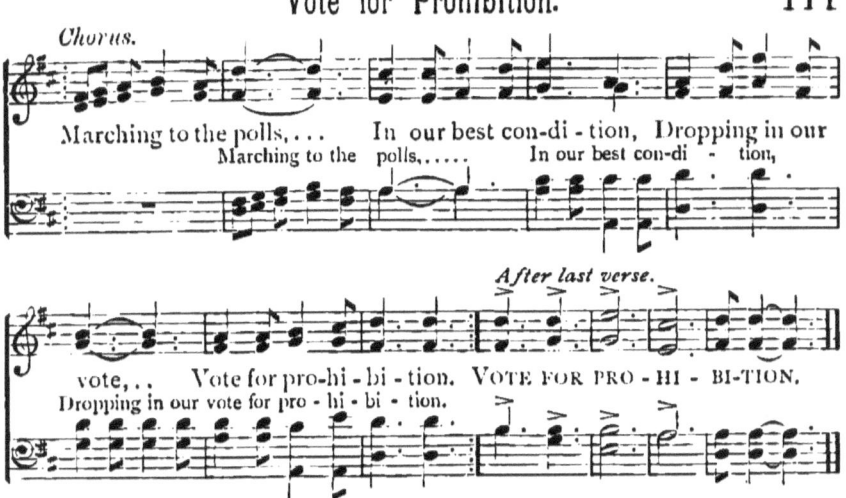

Note.—"You are not going to throw away your vote by voting for Prohibition, are you?" said one man to another, at the last election. "Yes, sir;" was the reply. "I am marching to the polls in my best condition. Nothing else will do for me to-day; so I shall vote for Prohibition."

Evening Shades.

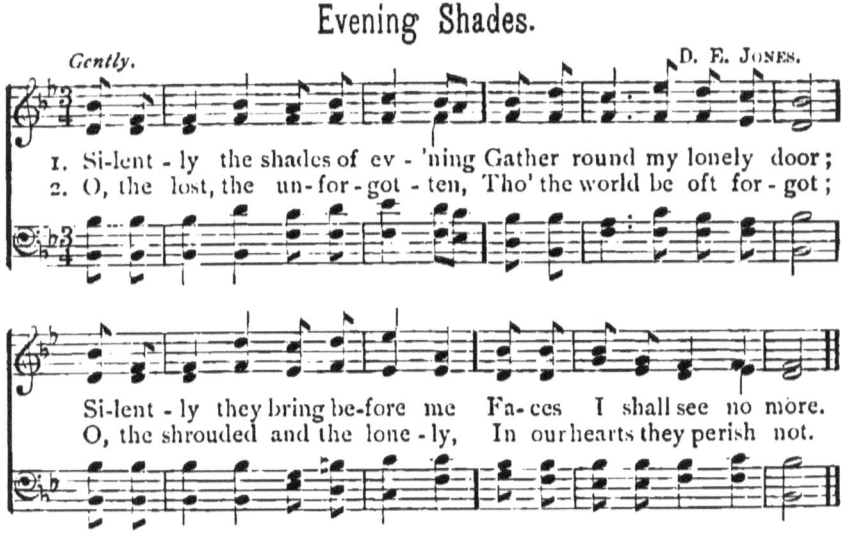

3 Living in the silent hours,
   Where our spirits only blend,
   They unlinked from earthly trouble,
   We still hoping for its end.

4 How such holy mem'ries cluster,
   Like the stars when storms are past;
   Pointing up to that fair haven,
   We may hope to gain at last.

112. Send out the Life-Lines.

MARIAN FROELICH.   ASA HULL.

1. The waves are ris-ing high, And sul-len breakers roar; A-bove the threat'ning sky Spreads over sea and shore. Far on the rag-ing main Full many a boat is tossed, Will they a har-bor gain, Or in the depths be lost?

2. Why stand ye on the strand, And nerveless view the scene, For souls with heart and hand The ocean's furrows gleam. Then bring the wreck'd ones in, Let them the past re-deem, And in the crown you'll win In heav'n bright stars will gleam.

Ritard.   *Refrain.*

Send, Send, Send out the life-lines! Send out the life-lines! Send out the life-lines! Sinking souls to save! Help! Help save the wreck'd ones!

COPYRIGHT, 1888, BY ASA HULL.

Send out the Life-Lines.

Help save the wreck'd ones! Save them from a yawn-ing grave!

Life's Battle-field.

R. TORRY.　　　　　　　　　　　　　　　ASA HULL.

1. Sol-diers on life's bat-tle-field, Be ye val-iant, bold and strong;
2. Hark! the bat-tle is be-gun! Ral-ly, Christians, for your King;

In the strife, with cheer-ful zeal, Urge the Temp'rance cause a-long.
For-ward, till the vic-t'ry's won, Till the shouts of tri-umph ring!

Chorus.

On-ward, on-ward to glo-ry! Yield not to the wi-ly foe;

Vic-t'ry and heav'n are before thee; Shout your triumph as you go!

3 Jesus calls us to the field!
　He will lead us evermore;
　'Neath His banner ne'er to yield,
　Till the mighty conflict's o'er.

4 Then, in yonder world of light
　We will lay our armor down,
　And 'mid throngs of angels bright,
　Each receive a starry crown.

3.
And shout aloud saloons must go!
Ye that have been their spoil;
Ye that have caused their wealth to grow,
E'en by your blood and hardy toil.
Saloons must go!

4.
Shout all aloud saloons must go!
Work for the glorious end;
Speak, sing and vote to overthrow,
Pray heav'n its holy aid to lend.
Saloons must go!

COPYRIGHT, 1888, BY ASA HULL.

116. Save my Boy To-night.

ELIZA M. SHERMAN. WM. J. KIRKPATRICK.

1. Ros-y glow the ta-pers In the bar-room bright, Where a boy is standing In their ru-by light; Bright, oh! bright their shining, Will he go or stay? Tell him of his dan-ger, Bid him flee a-way!

2. Red the wine is glowing In the glass to-night, And it gives no sig-nal Of its dead-ly blight; Hark! the sound of laughter— Mad, unmeaning joy! Warn him of his dan-ger, Save, oh, save my boy!

3. Ros-y glow the ta-pers In the bar-room bright, And a prayer is fall-ing On the air to-night: "Fa-ther, hear the plead-ing, Bring the sad heart joy; From the deadly wine-cup, Save, oh, save the boy."

Chorus.

Save, oh, save my darling, From the wine-cup's blight; Save, oh, save my dar-ling, Save my boy to-night! Save, oh, save my dar-ling,

COPYRIGHT, 1888, BY ASA HULL.

3 No money now for rum is spent,
   We spend it for our living:
   You ought to see the grand good things,
   Our well-fill'd pantry's giving.

4 The rent is paid, our home is sure,
   We even hope to buy it;
   If you don't know the worth of this,
   Why you had better try it.

COPYRIGHT, 1888, BY ASA HULL.

GOSPEL TEMPERANCE.

Silent Mercies.

W. E. PENNEY. ASA HULL.

1. Si-lent-ly as twilight shadows Fall when daylight fades a-way;
2. Si-lent-ly, but oh! how sweetly Comes the Spirit, full of grace;
3. Si-lent-ly as fall-ing snowflakes, Speed the white-winged angels down;

So the mer-cies of our Fa-ther, Come to bless us day by day.
Whisp'ring joy and hope and comfort, Pointing up to His dear face.
Cheering us in life's great bat-tle, Bringing some the victor's crown.

Chorus.

Si- lent-ly, so si- lent-ly, But still fraught with gracious pow'r,
Come the blessings of the Fa-ther To His children ev-'ry hour.

4 Silently as comes the starlight,
  Softly banishing night's gloom;
So the love of our dear Father
  Lights the passage to the tomb.

5 Silently, O blessed Spirit,
  Come and dwell in every heart;
Till we reach Thy glorious presence,
  And behold Thee as Thou art.

COPYRIGHT, 1883, BY ASA HULL.

The Rock of Ages.

LANTA WILSON SMITH.   ASA HULL.

1. When the tempest rag-es high, Cling to the Rock of A-ges;
2. In temp-ta-tion's try-ing hour, Cling to the Rock of A-ges;

When the an-gry waves roll by, Cling to the Rock of A-ges.
Sin will lose its lur-ing pow'r, When on the Rock of A-ges.

There is a ref-uge sure, That ev-er shall en-dure,
The tempter with his snare, Turns back in sore de-spair,

Where the soul shall rest se-cure, Safe on the Rock of A-ges.
If he finds you rest-ing there, Safe on the Rock of A-ges.

3.
When the sunshine lights the way,
  Cling to the Rock of Ages;
In prosperity's glad day,
  Cling to the Rock of Ages.
Though all the world seems bright,
Trust not its treach'rous light,
Lest you feel its with'ring blight,
  Cling to the Rock of Ages.

4.
In life's sorrow and its pain
  Cling to the Rock of Ages;
When your cherished hopes are slain,
  Cling to the Rock of Ages.
When hearts beat faint and slow,
Our work all done below,
Find, when we from earth shall go,
  Heav'n in the Rock of Ages.

COPYRIGHT, 1888, BY ASA HULL.

The Standard of Jesus wave.

1. Down from the ramparts of glory and might Ringeth the war-cry clear;
2. Fight 'gainst the princes of darkness and night, Powers of earth and sin;

Soldier, the order has come, you must fight, Take then the sword and spear.
Tho' they may rage, yet for God and the right Glory and vict'ry win.

Chorus.

Fight, for the God of bat-tles fight! True be your arm, and brave!
O - ver the ar - my's conquering host, Standard of Je - sus, wave!

3 Fierce though the heat of the battle's wild glare,
   Loud though the cannons roar,
Glimpses of crowns and of palms waving there,
   Promise a rest once more.—*Chorus.*

4 Then when the night ends the warfare and strife,
   Hear the Commander call:
Soldier and victor, thy prize endless life,
   Enter the banquet hall.—*Chorus.*

COPYRIGHT, 1884, BY ASA HULL.

Room for the Prodigal.

Rev. J. H. Martin.   T. Frank Allen.

1. Room for the prod-i-gal, mourning for sin; Room in the kingdom of God, let him in; Room in the mansions of glo-ry a-bove;
2. Sin-ner, re-turn from the paths thou hath trod, Walk in the ways of thy Fa-ther and God; Fol-low the foot-steps of Je-sus thy guide,

Chorus.

Room in the bo-som of Christ, full of love. Room for the prod-i-gal, mourn-ing for sin; Room for the prod-i-gal, O, let him in.
Trust in the blood of the once Cru-ci-fied.

3 Come unto Jesus for pardon and rest,
 Come in contrition and lean on His breast;
 Burdened with guilt, He will give thee release;
 Troubled with sorrow He'll fill thee with peace.—*Chorus.*

4 Loosed from the bondage of Satan and sin,
 Run in the race, and the victory win;
 Fight unto death, then thy armor lay down,
 Enter thy rest and receive a bright crown.—*Chorus.*

COPYRIGHT, 1884, BY ASA HULL.

Thanks be to God. 125

Sing a glad ho-san-na! Ho-san-na! ho-san-na! ho-san-na!
Sing ho-san-na!

Work for the Master.

Mrs. E. C. Ellsworth.   J. H. Tenney.

1. Ev - er let thy hand be bus - y, Lay the threads out one by one;
2. Nev - er heed the i - dlers round thee, Watchful be with pa-tient eye;
3. Hand and eye must work to-geth-er, Standing 'neath a light di - vine;

Ev - er ply time's ceaseless shuttle, Till life's work is no-bly done.
Mark thou well the no - ble pat-tern, And thy life - work beau-ti-fy.
Thou shalt bring a last-ing ser - vice, And the "Well done" shall be thine.

Chorus.

Work then for the blessed Mas-ter! He is with thee day by day;
Work then for the

Slow.

Be thou faith - ful to thy call-ing; Work a-way! yes, work a - way!
Be thou faithful

COPYRIGHT, 1884, BY ASA HULL.

126. The Sacred Stream.

Solo.—Allegretto. ASA HULL.

1. There is a stream, whose gen-tle flow Sup-plies the cit-y of...... our God;.... Life, love, and joy, still glid-ing through, And wa-t'ring our di-vine..... a-bode......
2. That sa-cred stream, Thine ho-ly word, That all our rag-ing fear.... con-trols;.... Sweet peace Thy prom-is-es... af-ford, And give new strength to faint-ing souls......
3. Loud may the troub-led o-cean roar; In sa-cred peace our souls... a-bide;.... While ev-'ry na-tion, ev-'ry shore, Trem-bles and dreads the swell-ing tide......

Full Chorus.

Life, love, and joy, still glid-ing through, And wa-t'ring our di-
Sweet peace Thy prom-is-es... af-ford, And give new strength to
While ev-'ry na-tion, ev-'ry shore, Trem-bles and dreads the

COPYRIGHT, 1879, BY ASA HULL.

The Sacred Stream. 127

vine.... a-bode, And wa-t'ring our... di-vine a-bode.
faint - ing souls, And give new strength to faint-ing souls.
swell - ing tide, Trem-bles and dreads the swell-ing tide.

America.

SAMUEL S. SMITH. HENRY CAREY.

1. My coun-try, 'tis of thee, Sweet land of lib-er-ty,
2. My na-tive coun-try! thee, Land of the no-ble free,

Of thee I sing; Land where my fa-thers died, Land of the
Thy name I love; I love thy rocks and rills, Thy woods and

pilgrim's pride, From ev-'ry mountain side Let free-dom ring.
tem-pled hills; My heart with rap-ture thrills Like that a-bove.

3 Let music swell the breeze,
And ring from all the trees
Sweet freedom's song!
Let mortal tongues awake;
Let all that breathe partake;
Let rocks their silence break;
The sound prolong!

4 Our fathers' God! to Thee,
Author of liberty,
To Thee we sing:
Long may our land be bright
With freedom's holy light;
Protect us by Thy might,
Great God, our King!

128. Peace, be Still!

M. A. Baker. — H. R. Palmer.

1. Master, the tempest is rag-ing, The billows are toss-ing high,
   The sky is o'ershadow'd with blackness, No shel-ter or help is nigh;
   "Car-est Thou not that we per-ish?" How canst Thou lie a-sleep,
   When each moment so madly is threat'ning A grave in the an-gry deep?

2. Master, with anguish of spir-it I bow in my grief to-day;
   The depths of my sad heart are troubled, Oh, waken and save, I pray:
   Tor-rents of sin and of an-guish Sweep o'er my sink-ing soul;
   And I per-ish! I per-ish! dear Master, O hast-en to take con-trol.

Chorus.

The winds and the waves shall obey my will, Peace,.. be still!..
Peace, be still! Peace, be still!

By permission of Dr. H. R. Palmer, owner of copyright.

Peace, be Still!

3 Master, the terror is over,
   The elements sweetly rest;
Earth's sun in the calm lake is mirror'd,
   And heaven's within my breast;
Linger, O blessed Redeemer,
   Leave me alone no more,
And with joy I shall make the blest harbor.
   And rest on the blissful shore.

130. Under His Wings.

JAMES NICHOLSON.   ASA HULL.

1. In God I have found a re-treat, Where I can se-cure-ly a-bide;
2. I dread not the ter-ror by night; No ar-row can harm me by day;
3. The pes-ti-lence walking a-bout, When darkness has set-tled a-broad,

No ref-uge nor rest so complete, And here I in-tend to re-side.
His shadow has covered me quite; My fears He has driven a-way.
Can nev-er com-pel me to doubt The presence and power of God.

Chorus.

O, what com-fort it brings, as my soul sweet-ly sings:

I am safe from all dan-ger while un-der His wing.

4 The wasting destruction at noon,
   No fearful foreboding can bring;
With Jesus my soul doth commune,
   His perfect salvation I sing.

5 A thousand may fall at my side,
   Ten thousand fall at my right hand;
Above me His wings are spread wide,
   Beneath them in safety I stand.

COPYRIGHT, 1872, BY ASA HULL.

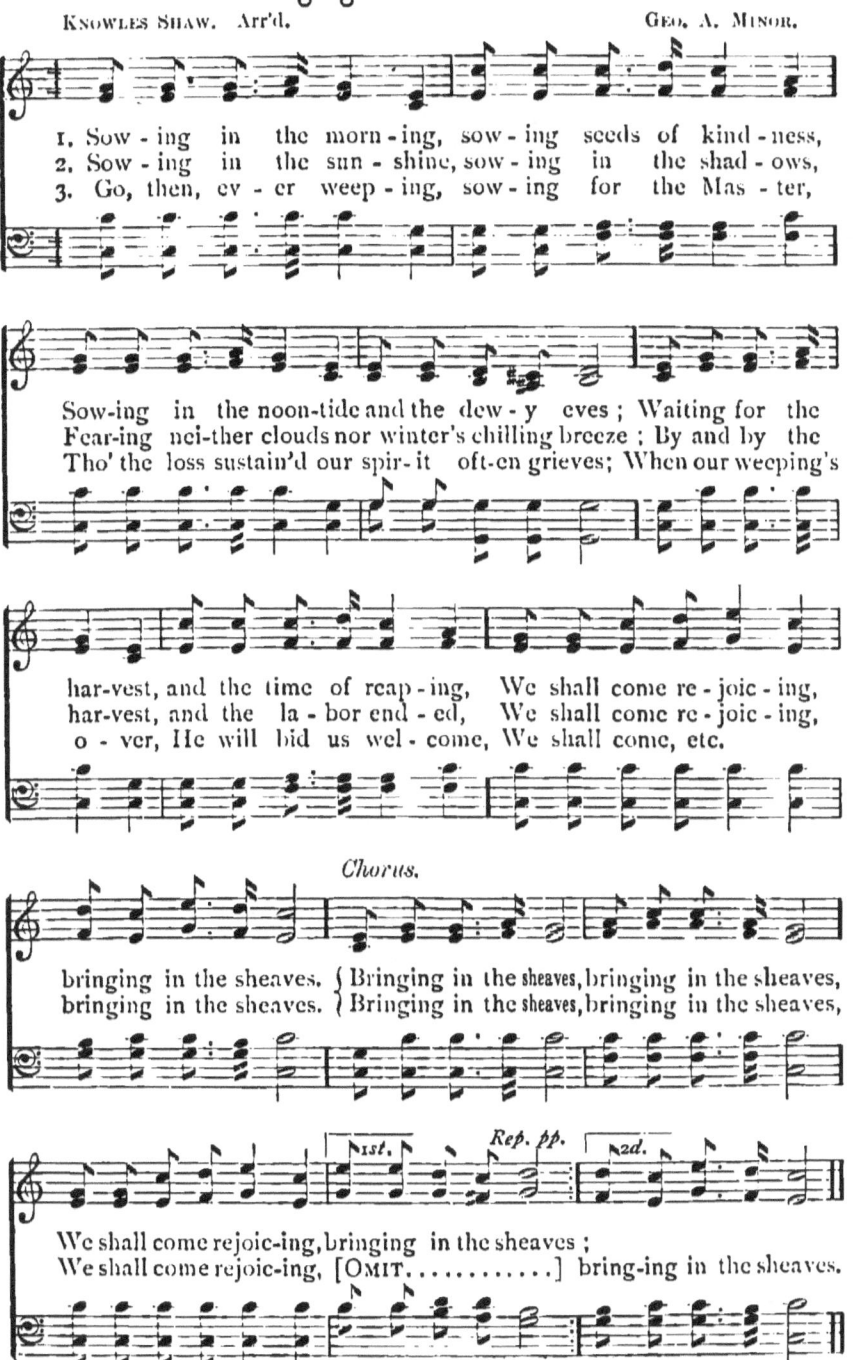

Better Further On. 133

Not too Fast.   Asa Hull.

1. A gentle breeze from Eden's land, Wafts o'er the stream a heav'nly song;
   They're singing on the shin-ing strand, That it's bet-ter fur-ther on.
2. I hear the soft, the glad re-frain, I catch the sound and then 'tis gone;
   They're singing o'er and o'er a-gain, "It is bet-ter fur-ther on."

Refrain.

"It is bet-ter,.... it is bet-ter,.... it is bet-ter,.... it is
further on,   further on,   further on,
bet-ter,.... It is bet-ter,.... it is bet-ter,.... it is
fur-ther on;   fur-ther on,   fur-ther on,
bet-ter, it is bet-ter, It is bet-ter fur-ther on."

3 By faith I look across the main,   4 Hope ever sings the self-same song,
   Where lov'd ones have already gone,   To cheer the pilgrim, worn and wan,
   Lo! they have caught the sweet refrain,   Tho' rough the road, and, may be, long,
   "It is better further on."   Yet, 'tis better further on.

COPYRIGHT, 1880, BY ASA HULL.

Scatter Seeds of Kindness.

Mrs. Albert Smith.   S. J. Vail.

1. Let us gath-er up the sunbeams, Ly-ing all a-round our path;
2. Strange we never prize the mu-sic 'Till the sweet-voic'd bird is flown!

Let us keep the wheat and ros-es, Cast-ing out the thorns and chaff;
Strange that we should slight the violets Till the love-ly flow'rs are gone!

Let us find our sweetest com-fort In the blessings of to-day,
Strange that summer skies and sunshine Nev-er seem one half so fair,

With a pa-tient hand re-mov-ing All the bri-ars from the way.
As when win-ter's snow-y pin-ions Shake the white down in the air.

Chorus.

Then scatter seeds of kindness, Then scatter seeds of kindness,

Scatter Seeds of Kindness.

3 If we knew the baby fingers,
   Pressed against the window pane,
   Would be cold and stiff to-morrow,—
   Never trouble us again,—
   Would the bright eyes of our darling
   Catch the frown upon our brow?—
   Would the prints of rosy fingers
   Vex us then as they do now?

4 Ah! those little ice-cold fingers,
   How they point the memories back
   To the hasty words and actions
   Strewn around our backward track!
   How these little hands remind us,
   As in snowy grace they lie,
   Not to scatter thorns, but roses,
   For our reaping by and by.

Heav'n is my Home.

3 Peace! O my troubled soul,
   Heav'n is my home;
   I soon shall reach the goal;
   Heav'n is my home:
   Swiftly the race I'll run,
   Yield up my crown to none;
   Forward! the prize is won;
   Heav'n is my home.

4 There, at my Saviour's side,
   Heav'n is my home;
   I shall be glorified;
   Heav'n is my home:
   There are the good and blest,
   Those I lov'd most and best;
   There, too, I soon shall rest;
   Heav'n is my home.

The Sheltering Rock. 137

Words and Music by W. J. KIRKPATRICK.

1. There's a firm, shelt'ring Rock, and a strong fortress tow'r, Where the weary and weak can renew failing pow'r, Where the tempted and care-laden spirit may fly,—
2. 'Tis a ref-uge and rest thro' the conflicts of life, 'Tis a balm to the soul, when dismayed in the strife; 'Tis a spring of salvation, a stream never dry,

Chorus.

O lead me to the Rock that is higher than I.
A never-failing Rock that is higher than I.
Lead me to the Rock, O lead me, Lead, O lead me to the Rock, Lead me to the Rock, O lead me, Lead me to the Rock that is higher than I.

3 'Tis my comfort and stay, my deliv'rer and joy,
When the heart is o'erwhelmed with the ills that annoy;
When the fierce sweeping tempest of sorrow is nigh,
O lead me to the Rock that is higher than I.

4 When the few joys of life are all flitting away,
Like the soft fading light at the closing of day,
When the shadow of death steals the light from my eye,
O lead me to the Rock that is higher than I,

COPYRIGHT, 1874, BY ASA HULL.

Let There be Light.

WILLIE WILDER.   ASA HULL.

1. Thro' heav'n's clear arch the echoes rang, As morning stars together sang;
2. From star to star the watchword flies; Each shouts it onward thro' the skies:
3. The sons of morn with lasting song, Will ev-er pass the word a-long;

And na-ture fresh from chaos woke, When on her ear the cho-rus broke,
From out the cha - os grim and black It speeds a-long its shin-ing track,
And waking men with rapture thrill, For, breaking o'er each eastern hill,

Duet.

As her Al-might - y Maker spoke, "Let there be light!".....
Till earth the ech - o answer'd back, "Let there be light!".....
The ear-ly dawn is shout-ing still, "Let there be light!".....

Chorus.

"Let there be light!"..... "Let there be light!"..... "Let there be
"Let there be light!"   "Let there be light!"

light!".... AND THERE WAS LIGHT.
"Let there be light!"

4.
The soul may feel the heavy blight,
Of deepest ignorance and night;
Yet may the densest cloud be riven,
And back the darkness may be driven
By that command which God hath given,
"Let there be light!"

COPYRIGHT, 1871, BY ASA HULL.

Refuge.

139

CHARLES WESLEY.   JOS. P. HOLBROOK.

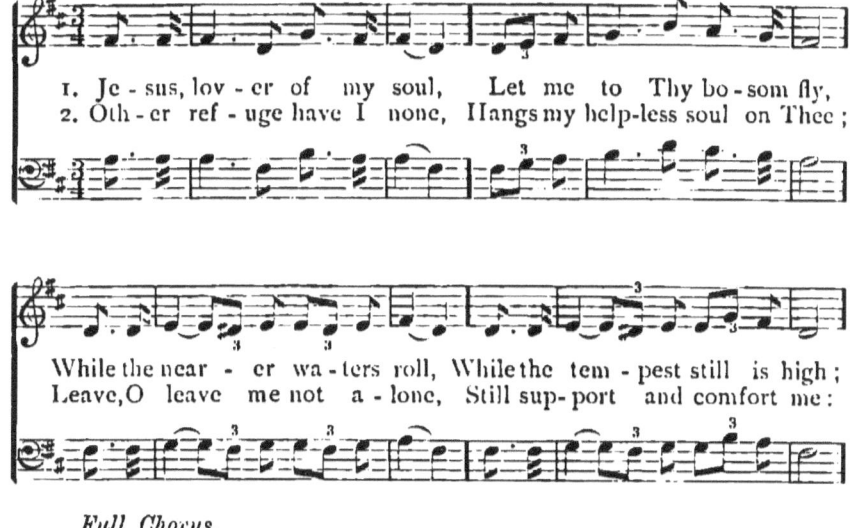

1. Jesus, lover of my soul, Let me to Thy bosom fly,
2. Other refuge have I none, Hangs my helpless soul on Thee;

While the nearer waters roll, While the tempest still is high;
Leave, O leave me not alone, Still support and comfort me:

Full Chorus.

Hide me, O my Saviour, hide, Till the storm of life is past;
All my trust on Thee is stayed, All my help from Thee I bring;

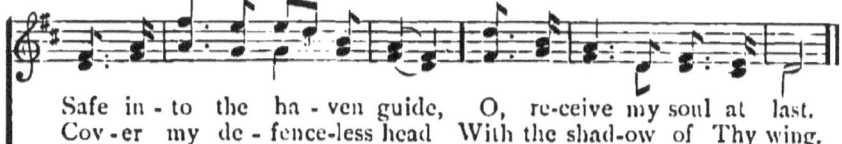

Safe into the haven guide, O, receive my soul at last.
Cover my defenceless head With the shadow of Thy wing.

3 Thou, O Christ, art all I want;
  More than all in Thee I find:
Raise the fallen, cheer the faint,
  Heal the sick, and lead the blind:
Just and holy is Thy name,
  I am all unrighteousness;
Vile, and full of sin I am,
  Thou art full of truth and grace.

4 Plenteous grace with Thee is found—
  Grace to cover all my sin:
Let the healing streams abound;
  Make me, keep me pure within.
Thou of life the Fountain art,
  Freely let me take of Thee;
Spring Thou up within my heart,
  Rise to all eternity.

140. All for Jesus!

Mary D James. — Mixed Voices. — Asa Hull.

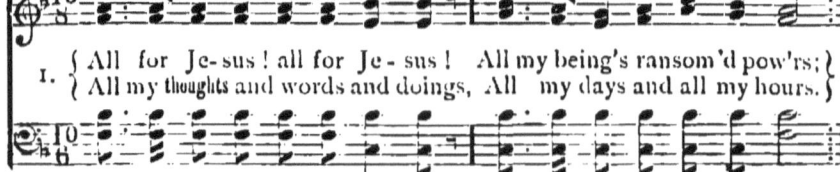

1. All for Je-sus! all for Je-sus! All my being's ransom'd pow'rs;
All my thoughts and words and doings, All my days and all my hours.

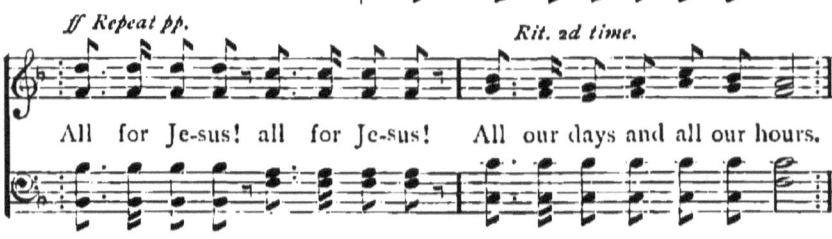

ff Repeat pp.   *Rit. 2d time.*

All for Je-sus! all for Je-sus! All our days and all our hours.

2.
Let my hands perform His bidding;
Let my feet run in His ways;
Let my eyes see Jesus only;
Let my lips speak forth His praise;
All for Jesus! all for Jesus!
Let my lips speak forth His praise;

3.
Worldlings prize their gems of beauty,
Cling to gilded toys of dust,
Boast of wealth, and fame, and pleasure;
Only Jesus will I trust.
Only Jesus! only Jesus!
Only Jesus will I trust.

4.
Since my eyes were fixed on Jesus,
I've lost sight of all beside,—
So enchained my spirit's vision,
Looking at the crucified.
All for Jesus! all for Jesus!
All for Jesus, crucified!

5.
O, what wonder! how amazing!
Jesus, glorious King of kings,
Deigns to call me His beloved,
Lets me rest beneath His wings.
All for Jesus! all for Jesus!
Resting now beneath His wings.

All for Jesus!

Mary D. James. — Male Voices. — Asa Hull.

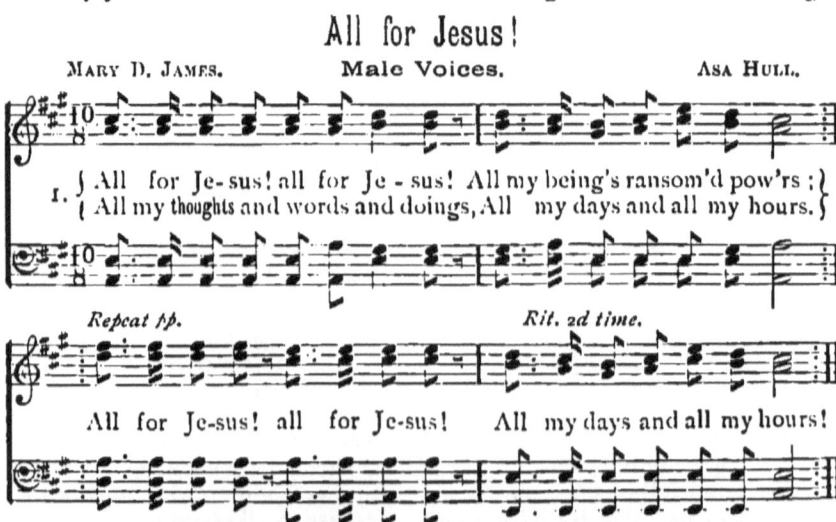

1. All for Je-sus! all for Je-sus! All my being's ransom'd pow'rs;
All my thoughts and words and doings, All my days and all my hours.

Repeat pp.   *Rit. 2d time.*

All for Je-sus! all for Je-sus! All my days and all my hours!

Copyright, 1873, 1877, and 1879, by Asa Hull.

Only Remembered.

3 Only the truth that in life I have spoken,
  Only the seed that on earth I have sown,
  These shall pass onward when I am forgotten,
  Fruits of the harvest, and what I have done.
   Cho.—Only remembered by what I have done.

4 O, when the Saviour shall make up His jewels,
  When the bright crowns of rejoicing are won,
  Then will His faithful and weary disciples
  All be remembered for what they have done.
   Cho.—Only remembered by what they have done.

COPYRIGHT, 1876, BY ASA HULL.

3 O the love of Christ is higher
    Than our aspirations are;
    And it bids each soul come nearer,
    Even me who strayed so far.
    Ref. Even me, yes! even me;
         Even me who strayed so far.
         Hallelujah! hallelujah!
         Even me who strayed so far.

4 O this love is everlasting,
    Naught has power to break the tie;
    One with Christ, I all inherit,
    I am His, yes! even I.
    Ref. Even I, yes! even I;
         I am His, yes! even I.
         Hallelujah! hallelujah!
         I am His, yes! even I.

Put on the Armor. 143

Mrs. E. C. Ellsworth.   J. H. Tenney.

1. Put on the ar-mor of our God, Be strong to do His will;
2. Put on the ar-mor, girt with truth, The work is not thine own;

Dare not go forth for once un-armed, Thy foes would do thee ill.
Bind to thy heart the law of God, Ful-filled by Christ a-lone.

Chorus.

Stand firm! stand firm, de-fy the foe! Thou in the Master's
Then stand! stand firm,

strength shall go, En-dur-ing to the end. Then stand! stand
Then stand! Then stand!

firm, de-fy the foe, En-dur-ing to the end.
stand firm,

3.
Put on the armor; shod with peace
Thy feet shall firm endure;
Tho' snares beset and thorns shall pierce,
He makes thy footsteps sure.

4.
Put on the armor; take thy shield,
Faith in the risen Lord;
Once pierced with darts still aimed at thee,
He conquers with a word.

COPYRIGHT, 1879, BY ASA HULL.

One Day Nearer Home.

Repeat pp. ad lib.
Near - er, near - er, One day near - er home......
Near- er, near- er, near- er, near-er, near-er home.

3.
Nearer home! yes, one day nearer,
To our Father's house on high,
To the green fields and the fountains
Of the land beyond the sky;
For the heav'ns grow brighter o'er us,
And the lamps hang in the dome,
And our tents are pitch'd still closer,
For we're one day nearer home.

4.
"One day nearer," sings the mar'ner,
As he glides the waters o'er,
While the light is softly dying
On his distant native shore;
Thus the Christian on life's ocean,
As his life-boat cuts the foam,
In the evening cries with rapture,
"I am one day nearer home."

Come, ye Disconsolate.

Solo or Duet. WEBBE.

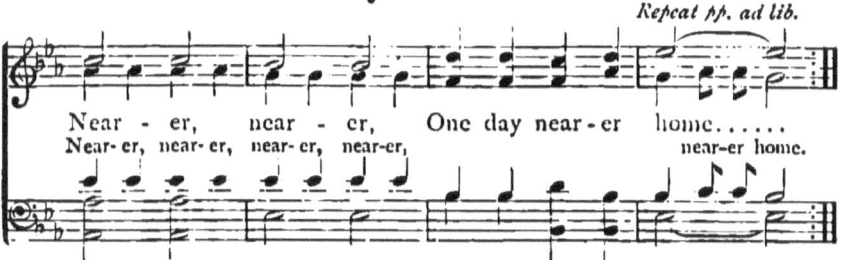

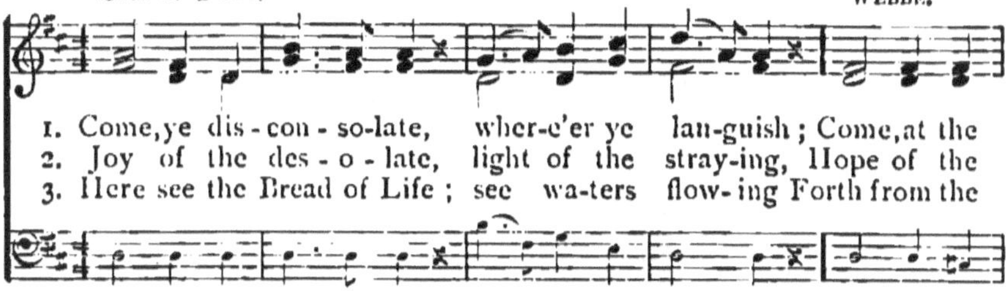
1. Come,ye dis - con - so-late, wher-e'er ye lan-guish; Come,at the
2. Joy of the des - o - late, light of the stray-ing, Hope of the
3. Here see the Bread of Life; see wa-ters flow- ing Forth from the

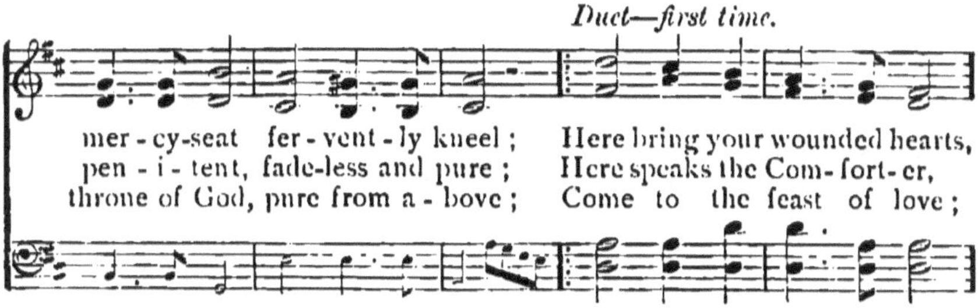
Duet—first time.
mer - cy-seat fer - vent - ly kneel; Here bring your wounded hearts,
pen - i - tent, fade-less and pure; Here speaks the Com- fort- er,
throne of God, pure from a - bove; Come to the feast of love;

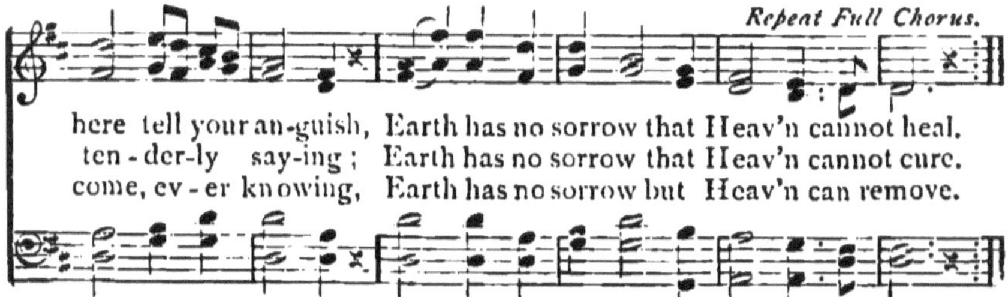
Repeat Full Chorus.
here tell your an-guish, Earth has no sorrow that Heav'n cannot heal.
ten - der-ly say-ing; Earth has no sorrow that Heav'n cannot cure.
come, ev - er knowing, Earth has no sorrow but Heav'n can remove.

148. Work, for the Night is Coming.

SIDNEY DYER.   Dr. L. MASON.

1. Work, for the night is com-ing, Work thro' the morning hours;
2. Work, for the night is com-ing, Work thro' the sun-ny noon;

Work while the dew is spark-ling, Work 'mid springing flow'rs;
Fill brightest hours with la-bor,— Rest comes sure and soon:

Work, when the day grows bright-er, Work in the glow-ing sun;
Give ev-'ry fly-ing min-ute Something to keep in store;

Work, for the night is com-ing, When man's work is done.
Work, for the night is com-ing, When man works no more.

3.
Work, for the night is coming,
  Under the sunset skies;
While their bright tints are glowing,
  Work, for daylight flies;
Work, till the last beam fadeth,
  Fadeth to shine no more;
Work, while the night is dark'ning,
  When man's work is o'er.

4.
Work, for the night is coming,
  Work, while the fields are white;
Work, for thy sands are running,
  Work, while hopes are bright;
Gather thy sheaves of morning;
  Rest not thy hand at noon;
Labor and strive till ev'ning;
  Rest, when daylight's gone,

REVISED ODES
OF THE
INDEPENDENT ORDER OF GOOD TEMPLARS

AUTHORISED BY B. F. PARKER, R. W. G. S.

COPYRIGHT, 1888, BY B. F. PARKER.

SUBORDINATE ODES.

No. 1. Opening, No. 1.

L. MASON. Arr'd.

Friends of Temp'rance, welcome here, Cheerful are our hearts to-day;

Tell us, we would glad-ly hear How our cause speeds on its way.

Here we pledge ourselves a-new, Not to touch the drunkard's drink;

Prov-ing faith-ful, prov-ing true, We will from no du-ty shrink.

150 No. 2.   Opening, No. 2.
                                                   GEO. N. ALLEN.

1. Thy mer-cy, Lord, we hum-bly seek, Thy blessing from a-bove;
2. O let Thy blessing here descend To give our work suc-cess;
3. May Temp'rance lead them with delight To search Thy ho-ly word;

To Thee we now all pow'r as-cribe, Thou source of life and love.
May man-y take and keep our pledge, And seek true hap-pi-ness.
And may they feel Thy sav-ing pow'r, And own Thee for their Lord.

No. 3.   Initiation, No. 1.
[Admit them.]   WM. B. BRADBURY.

{ Welcome, welcome to our Or-der, We shall need your help and care; }
{ In the harvest-fields of Temp'rance, You shall have a rightful share. }

Welcome, welcome, welcome, welcome, Heaven bless you! is our prayer;

Welcome, welcome, welcome, welcome, Heaven bless you! is our prayer.

No. 4.   Initiation, No. 2.   (Above Tune.)

Welcome, ye whose hearts are beating   All the joys of union feel.
   High with hope and love and zeal: ‖: Welcome, welcome, (4 *times*)
Here with kindred spirits meeting,   Welcome to our brotherhood. :‖

2 May our circle ne'er be broken
 By the tempter's subtle pow'r ;
 Here may friendships ne'er be severed,
 Till we reach life's closing hour.

3 Then, though earthly ties be sundered
 In the silence of the tomb ;
 May we be again united
 In the land of fadeless bloom.

2 The weak and the strong can join in the fight;
Can strive against wrong, and live for the right;
Through mutual assistance we mighty shall grow,
To offer resistance and conquer the foe.

3 We aim to release the victims of wrong,
Regardless of race, of nation, or tongue;
The foe may seem strongest yet we will assail,
For truth shall stand longest, and right shall prevail.

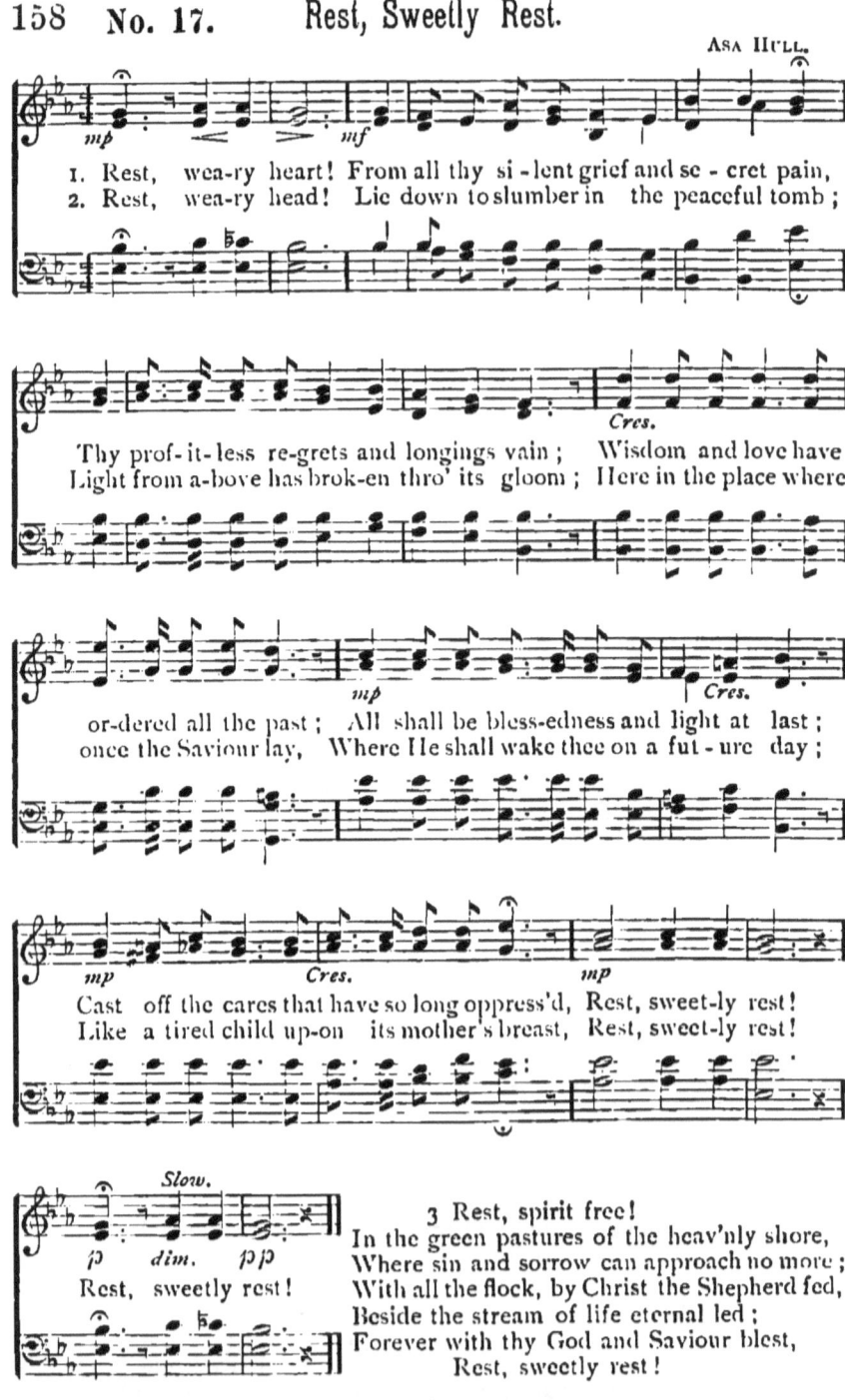

INDEX OF TUNES.

ALL for Jesus	140
America	127
Ask me not to sip the wine	72
Awake, Columbia, awake	37
Away with the saloon	114
Away with the wine cup	50
BATTLE Hymn, Women's Crusade	83
Beacon Lights are Shining	16
Be Men of Action	77
Be true to your manhood	86
Better further on	133
Be up and doing	29
Boundless love	142
Bravely marching on	118
Break the chain	42
Bringing in the sheaves	131
CAPTIVITY and Ruin	115
Charity	95
Cheer up, you'll win the day	54
Cold water for me	41
Come, ye Disconsolate	147
Courage, Brother	74
DARE to say No	18
Deeds of kindness	76
Don't say it	94
Down with the Brake	79
Down with the Traffic	90
Drink is raging	101
EVENING Shades	111
GOD is marching on	78
God speed the right	25
Go in Jesus' name	106
Greeting Refrain	65
HEAVEN is my home	135
Home! Sweet Home	23
I MAY not be a prophet	46
In God we trust	58
JOYOUS Tidings	89
KEEP it rolling	48
Keep out of the gutter	36
Keep your record clean	34
LABOR on	5
Life's Battle-field	113
Let there be Light	138
MARCHING on to Victory	12
Mother's praying for you	82
My wife and I	117
NOTHING but leaves	85
ODES, I. O. Good Templars	149-158
Oh come, and join us	11
One day nearer home	146
Only Remembered	141
On the field of battle	47
On to meet the foe	15
O the good we may be doing	20
Our noble Temperance Girls	92
Our Ship of State	28
PAPA darling, do not leave us	104
Peace, be still	128
Prohibition Song	81
Prohibition. What is it?	22
Push the cause along	68
Put on the armor	143
RAISE aloft the Temperance Banner	91
Rally round our Banner	70
Refuge	139
Rescue the erring	13
Right against the wrong	44
Right over wrong	102
Ring out the notes of warning	35
Ring the Joy-bells	40
Room for the prodigal	123
SALOONS must go	7
Save my Boy to-night	116
Scatter seeds of kindness	134
Send out the life-lines	112
Shout it through the Valley	21
Shun all liquid fire	49
Shun the Cup	31
Sign the Pledge to-day	26
Silent mercies	119
Singing all the day	122
Sing on, sing sweetly on	136
Songs of Faith	145
So will I comfort thee	71
Sound the Battle cry	27
Sparkling and bright	57
Sparkling Fountain	105
Straight for Prohibition	8
TEMPERANCE Marseilles	108
Thanks be to God	124
The Banner of Temperance	96
The Cross and Banner	63
The Danger Signal	9
The day is breaking	62
The glad Good-bye	17
The glorious battle-ground	56
The golden year	59

160   INDEX OF TUNES.

The happy days gone by	100	Trust in God and do right	80
The Jubilee of Temperance	69	UNDER His wings	130
The light from home	38–39	Unfurl the Temperance Banner	52
The Lord will provide	75	VICTORY at last	4
The lost is found	14	Vote as you pray	3
The Loyal Legion	19	Vote as you pray (male voices)	43
The poisonous cup	33	Vote for Prohibition	110
There's a ring to our cheer	88	Vote it out of Existence	87
There's hope for thee	32	WALK in the light	132
The Rock of Ages	120	Wave the Temperance Banner	24
The Sacred Stream	126	We'll conquer or die	51
The Sheltering Rock	137	We'll triumph by and by	10
The social glass	66	We will work on	84
The Standard of Jesus wave	121	What are you sowing?	6
The Temperance Army	45	When the mists have cleared away	144
The Temperance Call	61	Will you take the social glass?	67
The Temperance Warfare	64	Work for the Master	125
The Voice of Truth	73	Work, for the night is coming	148
The wife's prayer	98	YE brave men, to the rescue	30
The writing on the wall	60	Yield not to temptation	55
Toil away	53		

MALE QUARTETTES.

ALL for Jesus	140	Sign the Pledge to-day	26
Awake, Columbia, awake!	37	Straight for Prohibition	8
BREAK the chain	42	THE light from home	38
DOWN with the traffic	90	The Temperance Warfare	64
KEEP it rolling	48	The writing on the wall	60
Keep out of the gutter	36	There's a ring to our cheer	88
LABOR on	5	UNFURL the Temperance Banner	52
PROHIBITION—what is it?	22	VOTE as you pray	43
Push the cause along	68	Vote for Prohibition	110
RIGHT against the wrong	44	Vote it out of existence	87
SALOONS must go	7	WAVE the Temperance Banner	24

GOSPEL HYMNS, FIRST LINES.

A GENTLE breeze from Eden's land	133	O the love of Christ is boundless	142
All for Jesus! All for Jesus!	140	PUT on the armor of our God	143
COME, ye disconsolate, where'er ye	147	ROOM for the prodigal mourning	123
DOWN from the ramparts of glory	121	SILENTLY as twilight shadows	119
EVER let thy hand be busy	125	Sing on, my soul, thy mission prove	136
I'M but a stranger here	135	So will I comfort thee	71
In God I have found a retreat	130	Sowing in the morning, sowing	131
In some way or other	75	THANKS be to God for the vict'ry	124
I sing of Jesus' wondrous love	122	There is a stream whose gentle	126
JESUS, lover of my soul	139	There's a firm shelt'ring Rock	137
LET us gather up the sunbeams	134	Thro' heav'n's clear arch the echoes	138
MASTER, the tempest is raging	128	UP and away like the dew of the	141
My country, 'tis of thee	127	WALK in the light, the Lord	132
NOTHING but leaves, the Spirit	85	When the mists have rolled in	144
O'ER the hills the sun is setting	146	When the tempest rages high	120
O songs of faith that pilgrims sing	145	Work, for the night is coming	148

www.ingramcontent.com/pod-product-compliance
Lightning Source LLC
Chambersburg PA
CBHW030435190426
43202CB00036B/866